# Autumn
# Rambles

*New England*

D1166245

# Autumn Rambles

## *New England*

### An Explorer's Guide to the Best Fall Colors

*Michael & Mark Tougias*

**HUNTER**

HUNTER PUBLISHING, INC.
130 Campus Drive
Edison NJ 08818-7816, USA
Tel (732) 225 1900; Fax (732) 417 1744
E-mail: hunterpub@emi.net
Web site: www.hunterpublishing.com

1220 Nicholson Road
Newmarket, Ontario L3Y 7V1, CANADA
Tel (800) 399 6858; Fax (800) 363 2665

ISBN 1-55650-810-7

© 1998 Michael & Mark Tougias

*Cover: Autumn Colors oil painting by Mark Tougias*
*All interior illustrations by Mark Tougias*
*Maps by the authors*

# About the Authors

Michael Tougias writes on a wide range of topics, including history, nature, gardening and travel.

Michael frequently gives slide presentations about special historic and natural places in New England. Whenever possible, he volunteers for conservation work in an effort to save more open spaces. He is the author of *Nature Walks In Eastern Massachusetts, Quiet Places in Massachusetts, Nature Walks in Central Massachusetts, A Taunton River Journey, Exploring The Hidden Charles, Country Roads of Massachusetts, New England Wild Places, More Nature Walks in Eastern Massachusetts,* and *Cape Cod in the Words of Thoreau and Beston.* His first novel, *Until I Have No Country,* was published in 1996 and is set in Colonial New England during King Philip's Indian War. He has also published *Recreation Maps & Guides to Cape Cod, Hidden Quabbin, Rockport & Gloucester* and the *Southern Berkshires.* If you are interested in his publications or slide presentations, send a self-addressed stamped envelope to Michael Tougias, P.O. Box 72, Norfolk, MA 02056.

Mark Tougias is a well-known artist who lives in northern Vermont. His landscape paintings have appeared and won recognition in many galleries and juried exhibitions throughout New England. He is a member of the Northern Vermont Artist, the Southern Vermont Art Center in Manchester, and the North Shore Art Association of Gloucester, MA. Much of his inspiration is drawn from the surrounding beauty of the Green Mountain State. He is currently represented by, among others, the Blue Heron Gallery in Wellfleet, MA, the Clarke Gallery in Stowe, VT, the Silver Wing Art Gallery in Jeffersonville, VT, and the Blue Heron Art Gallery in Burlington, VT. Mark may be contacted at P.O. Box 31, Fairfield, VT 05455.

## Visit Our Web Site!

*For complete information about the hundreds of
other travel guides and language courses
offered by Hunter Publishing, visit us online at:*
**www.hunterpublishing.com**

Dedication

*With love to our sister, Lynn*

# Contents

INTRODUCTION . . . . . . . . . . . . . . . . . . . . . . . . . . 1
*Autumn In New England*. . . . . . . . . . . . . . . . . . . . . 3
   How, When & Where . . . . . . . . . . . . . . . . . . . . . 3
   A Few Tips . . . . . . . . . . . . . . . . . . . . . . . . . . 5
   Peepers' Hot Lines . . . . . . . . . . . . . . . . . . . . . . 6

CONNECTICUT . . . . . . . . . . . . . . . . . . . . . . . . . . 13
*The Quiet Corner, Northeast Connecticut* . . . . . . . . 15
   Canterbury . . . . . . . . . . . . . . . . . . . . . . . . . 15
   Brooklyn . . . . . . . . . . . . . . . . . . . . . . . . . . 16
   Pomfret . . . . . . . . . . . . . . . . . . . . . . . . . . 18
   Woodstock . . . . . . . . . . . . . . . . . . . . . . . . 20
*The Litchfield Hills, Northwest Connecticut* . . . . . . 23
   Litchfield . . . . . . . . . . . . . . . . . . . . . . . . . . 23
   Bantam Village . . . . . . . . . . . . . . . . . . . . . . . 26
   New Preston . . . . . . . . . . . . . . . . . . . . . . . . 27
   New Milford . . . . . . . . . . . . . . . . . . . . . . . . 28
   Kent . . . . . . . . . . . . . . . . . . . . . . . . . . . . 29
   Sharon . . . . . . . . . . . . . . . . . . . . . . . . . . . 31
   Salisbury . . . . . . . . . . . . . . . . . . . . . . . . . . 32
   North Canaan . . . . . . . . . . . . . . . . . . . . . . . 33
   East Canaan . . . . . . . . . . . . . . . . . . . . . . . . 33

RHODE ISLAND . . . . . . . . . . . . . . . . . . . . . . . . . 37
*The Hills of Southwestern Rhode Island* . . . . . . . . . 39
       *to Narragansett Bay*
   West Greenwich . . . . . . . . . . . . . . . . . . . . . . 40
   Exeter . . . . . . . . . . . . . . . . . . . . . . . . . . . 42
   Rockville . . . . . . . . . . . . . . . . . . . . . . . . . . 43
   Hope Valley & Kingston . . . . . . . . . . . . . . . . . 44
   Richmond . . . . . . . . . . . . . . . . . . . . . . . . . 45
   North Kingstown . . . . . . . . . . . . . . . . . . . . . 47
   Wickford . . . . . . . . . . . . . . . . . . . . . . . . . . 48

MASSACHUSETTS. . . . . . . . . . . . . . . . . . . . . . . . . . 51
*The Hills of Central Massachusetts* . . . . . . . . . . . . . 53
    Ware . . . . . . . . . . . . . . . . . . . . . . . . . . . . . . 54
    Belchertown & Pelham . . . . . . . . . . . . . . . . . . . . 54
    New Salem . . . . . . . . . . . . . . . . . . . . . . . . . . 55
    Petersham . . . . . . . . . . . . . . . . . . . . . . . . . . 58
    Phillipston . . . . . . . . . . . . . . . . . . . . . . . . . . 59
    West Brookfield . . . . . . . . . . . . . . . . . . . . . . . 60
*A Southern Berkshire Loop* . . . . . . . . . . . . . . . . . . 63
    Tyringham & Monterey . . . . . . . . . . . . . . . . . . . 63
    Great Barrington & Ashley Falls . . . . . . . . . . . . . 66
    South Egremont . . . . . . . . . . . . . . . . . . . . . . . 67
    Stockbridge . . . . . . . . . . . . . . . . . . . . . . . . . 69

VERMONT . . . . . . . . . . . . . . . . . . . . . . . . . . . . . . 71
*Southern Vermont* . . . . . . . . . . . . . . . . . . . . . . . 73
    Brattleboro . . . . . . . . . . . . . . . . . . . . . . . . . . 74
    Newfane . . . . . . . . . . . . . . . . . . . . . . . . . . . 75
    Townshend & Grafton . . . . . . . . . . . . . . . . . . . 76
    Jamaica . . . . . . . . . . . . . . . . . . . . . . . . . . . . 77
    Bondville . . . . . . . . . . . . . . . . . . . . . . . . . . . 78
    Manchester . . . . . . . . . . . . . . . . . . . . . . . . . 79
    Dorset . . . . . . . . . . . . . . . . . . . . . . . . . . . . . 80
    Arlington . . . . . . . . . . . . . . . . . . . . . . . . . . . 81
    Shaftsbury . . . . . . . . . . . . . . . . . . . . . . . . . . 82
    Bennington . . . . . . . . . . . . . . . . . . . . . . . . . 82
    Wilmington . . . . . . . . . . . . . . . . . . . . . . . . . 83
*Central Vermont Loop* . . . . . . . . . . . . . . . . . . . . . 87
    Northfield Falls . . . . . . . . . . . . . . . . . . . . . . . 87
    Brookfield . . . . . . . . . . . . . . . . . . . . . . . . . . 89
    Bethel . . . . . . . . . . . . . . . . . . . . . . . . . . . . . 90
    Pittsfield . . . . . . . . . . . . . . . . . . . . . . . . . . . 90
    Plymouth Union, Ludlow & Bridgewater . . . . . . . . 91
    Woodstock . . . . . . . . . . . . . . . . . . . . . . . . . . 92
    South Royalton . . . . . . . . . . . . . . . . . . . . . . . 93
    Tunbridge . . . . . . . . . . . . . . . . . . . . . . . . . . 94
    Chelsea . . . . . . . . . . . . . . . . . . . . . . . . . . . . 95

# Contents

Barre . . . . . . . . . . . . . . . . . . . . . . . . . . . . . . . . . 95
*Mount Mansfield Loop, Northern Vermont* . . . . . . . 99
  Stowe . . . . . . . . . . . . . . . . . . . . . . . . . . . . . . 99
  Jeffersonville . . . . . . . . . . . . . . . . . . . . . . . . 102
  Waterville . . . . . . . . . . . . . . . . . . . . . . . . . . 104
  Fairfield . . . . . . . . . . . . . . . . . . . . . . . . . . . 105
  St. Albans . . . . . . . . . . . . . . . . . . . . . . . . . . 106
  Westford . . . . . . . . . . . . . . . . . . . . . . . . . . . 107
  Jericho . . . . . . . . . . . . . . . . . . . . . . . . . . . . 108
  Underhill . . . . . . . . . . . . . . . . . . . . . . . . . . 109
  Cambridge . . . . . . . . . . . . . . . . . . . . . . . . . 110
  Morrisville . . . . . . . . . . . . . . . . . . . . . . . . . 110
*Northeast Kingdom* . . . . . . . . . . . . . . . . . . . . . . 113
  Hardwick . . . . . . . . . . . . . . . . . . . . . . . . . . 115
  East Craftsbury . . . . . . . . . . . . . . . . . . . . . . 116
  Irasburg . . . . . . . . . . . . . . . . . . . . . . . . . . . 117
  Barton . . . . . . . . . . . . . . . . . . . . . . . . . . . . 120
  Glover . . . . . . . . . . . . . . . . . . . . . . . . . . . . 121

NEW HAMPSHIRE . . . . . . . . . . . . . . . . . . . . . . . . 123
*Along the Connecticut River,* . . . . . . . . . . . . . . . . 125
    *Southern New Hampshire*
  Westmoreland Depot . . . . . . . . . . . . . . . . . . 126
  Walpole . . . . . . . . . . . . . . . . . . . . . . . . . . . 126
  Drewsville . . . . . . . . . . . . . . . . . . . . . . . . . 127
  Bellows Falls . . . . . . . . . . . . . . . . . . . . . . . . 128
  Charlestown . . . . . . . . . . . . . . . . . . . . . . . . 129
  Cornish . . . . . . . . . . . . . . . . . . . . . . . . . . . 130
  Hanover . . . . . . . . . . . . . . . . . . . . . . . . . . . 132
*Monadnock Region, Southern New Hampshire* . . . . 135
  Keene . . . . . . . . . . . . . . . . . . . . . . . . . . . . 137
  Jaffery . . . . . . . . . . . . . . . . . . . . . . . . . . . . 137
  Hancock . . . . . . . . . . . . . . . . . . . . . . . . . . 140
  Peterborough . . . . . . . . . . . . . . . . . . . . . . . 142
  Dublin . . . . . . . . . . . . . . . . . . . . . . . . . . . 145
  Harrisville . . . . . . . . . . . . . . . . . . . . . . . . . 146
  Nelson . . . . . . . . . . . . . . . . . . . . . . . . . . . . 147

*The Kancamagus Highway* . . . . . . . . . . . . . . . . . . 149
  Lincoln . . . . . . . . . . . . . . . . . . . . . . . . . . 151
MAINE . . . . . . . . . . . . . . . . . . . . . . . . . . . . . . 153
 *Southern Maine Ramble* . . . . . . . . . . . . . . . . . 155
  Standish & Sebago . . . . . . . . . . . . . . . . . . . . 156
  Bridgton . . . . . . . . . . . . . . . . . . . . . . . . . 158
  Fryeburg . . . . . . . . . . . . . . . . . . . . . . . . . 159
  Hiram . . . . . . . . . . . . . . . . . . . . . . . . . . . 160
  Porter . . . . . . . . . . . . . . . . . . . . . . . . . . . 161
 *The Kennebec River Valley* . . . . . . . . . . . . . . . . 165
  Bingham to The Forks & Beyond . . . . . . . . . . . 165
  Wyman Lake (Moscow & Bingham) . . . . . . . . . . 167
  Jackman . . . . . . . . . . . . . . . . . . . . . . . . . 170
  Hinckley . . . . . . . . . . . . . . . . . . . . . . . . . 171
  Norridgewock . . . . . . . . . . . . . . . . . . . . . . 171
 *Coastal Maine, Penobscot Peninsula* . . . . . . . . . . 173
  Blue Hill . . . . . . . . . . . . . . . . . . . . . . . . . 175
  Castine . . . . . . . . . . . . . . . . . . . . . . . . . . 177
  Stonington . . . . . . . . . . . . . . . . . . . . . . . . 179

# Maps

The Quiet Corner . . . . . . . . . . . . . . . . . . . . . . . . . 14
The Litchfield Hills . . . . . . . . . . . . . . . . . . . . . . . . 24
The Hills of Southwestern Rhode Island . . . . . . . . . . . 38
The Hills of Central Massachusetts . . . . . . . . . . . . . . . 52
A Southern Berkshire Loop . . . . . . . . . . . . . . . . . . . 64
Southern Vermont . . . . . . . . . . . . . . . . . . . . . . . . 72
Central Vermont Loop . . . . . . . . . . . . . . . . . . . . . . 88
Mount Mansfield Loop . . . . . . . . . . . . . . . . . . . . . 100
The Northeast Kingdom . . . . . . . . . . . . . . . . . . . . 114
Along The Connecticut River . . . . . . . . . . . . . . . . . 124
Monadnock Region . . . . . . . . . . . . . . . . . . . . . . . 136
The Kancamagus Highway . . . . . . . . . . . . . . . . . . . 150
Southern Maine . . . . . . . . . . . . . . . . . . . . . . . . . 155
Kennebec River Valley . . . . . . . . . . . . . . . . . . . . . 166
Coastal Maine . . . . . . . . . . . . . . . . . . . . . . . . . . 174

# Introduction

Where does one begin to tell of the great New England that we know, love and grew up in? Where does one "send" another, foreigner or neighbor, to find its beauty and to see and feel its grandeur? Having lived in New England all our lives, we knew too many places to go, too many places to tell about, too many wonderful autumn trails. And it was no surprise to either of us as we traveled the roads researching the book that there were countless more.

The challenges of choosing only 15 routes in six states were many. Besides our first objective of finding inspiring and varied landscapes coupled with places of interest, we knew that the roads we suggest must be in good shape and that directions should be easy. We offer a combination of well-known and not-so-well-known routes which, hopefully, fulfill our goal of suggesting and describing some of the best autumn experiences available in New England. We describe the routes in various ways, give directions and offer some of the nuts and bolts about travel in the area, including a list of fairs, festivals, places of interest, accommodations and important telephone numbers in the back of each chapter. We do not make gallant attempts to express the beauty of the place, but leave that up to the reader. We tell you only where you might find it.

We do not propose that travelers follow our routes and stops to the last letter. There are scores of places on or near these routes – hidden side roads, hiking trails, shops, scenic areas and historic sites – which are not mentioned, or perhaps only hinted at, in the text. Based on your travel needs and interests, make your own itinerary with this book as a reference. Mainly, get out and have a good time... and certainly, while you're on the road, follow the beat of your own drummer.

# Autumn in New England

## How, When & Where

Autumn is the season when New England shows off its best side. It seems as if the trees know they will soon lose their leaves, so they send them off in a blaze of color. Oak, maple, dogwood, aspen, beech and birch turn from a uniform green to distinctive hues of scarlet, orange, yellow and maroon. And the evergreens deserve credit, too, for they give the contrast and darker background that makes the deciduous trees seem all the brighter. As the shorter days and cooler weather cause the trees to stop producing chlorophyll (which has a dominant green color), the other pigments in the leaves begin to show through. In effect, the deciduous trees slow down at the end of the season, storing food in the roots and the leave's food-making work is over. Different varieties of trees turn different colors and it is this glorious combination that makes autumn so special. Although the different species of trees are responsible for the color, equally important (from a visual perspective) is the lay of the land. It is the hills and valleys that provide the vistas where a wide array of brilliant hues are splashed before us.

In open meadows all across the countryside, wildflowers add their beauty to the fall. Yellow tones of goldenrod, pink and purple Joe-Pye weed and violet astors seem to enjoy the last strong rays of the sun. Even one of the conifers, the cone-bearing tamarack, gets in on the act, when its lacy foliage turns yellow before dropping off. Migrating birds and butterflies touch down for a rest on their way south and hawks ride the thermals above ridgetops as they, too, head for warmer weather. All the while, the combination of cool nights and shorter days keeps the deciduous trees on their march toward peak color.

Although fall's glory can be enjoyed throughout most of the United States, New England is recognized as the prime "leaf-peeping" region with the most vivid colors. From Maine to Rhode Island, the area boasts the most dramatic colors because of the cool nights and the tree species that grow there.

Autumn officially begins on September 23rd, the date of the autumnal equinox, when day and night are of equal length. It ends on December 22nd, but by that time the leaves have long since fallen. The trick in enjoying the foliage transformation is to time your viewing to coincide with peak or near-peak color.

The first hints of color usually start in the mountains of Maine, New Hampshire and Vermont as early as the first of September and usually reach their peak at the end of the month and the beginning of October. This rainbow of turning foliage follows the Appalachian chain southward into the Berkshires of Massachusetts and the Litchfield Hills of Connecticut. By mid- to late October, the procession of colors has spread eastward toward Rhode Island and the coastal areas of southern New England.

Some of the most eye-catching color is supplied by a handful of trees. Maples provide more widespread, vivid beauty than any other tree. Sugar maples can be scarlet, yellow or orange, while swamp maples are brilliant red and are often the first tree to announce autumn's arrival. Dogwood and sumac are predominantly red, and birches, aspen, hickory and beeches usually have yellow or golden leaves. Oaks tend to first turn a rust color and then quickly show deeper shades of brown.

Certain areas of New England are "hotspots" for foliage rambles. These include the White Mountains of New Hampshire, the Green Mountains of central Vermont and the Berkshires in western Massachusetts. The main routes through these regions can get crowded with leaf peepers but, surprisingly, nearby back roads are often free of traffic. Sometimes getting "lost" on a country road is the best way to see fall color, second only to walking through the forest itself.

There are hidden pockets of New England that receive far fewer visitors than the popular tourist areas, yet the color and scenery can be equally dramatic. In New Hampshire, the southwestern portion of the state is often overlooked, and in Massachusetts, the central region surrounding giant Quabbin Reservoir is inviting to those who love a country road. Connecticut's "Quiet Corner," the northeastern section, is still relatively unspoiled and has wonderful foliage in October.

Coastal areas are usually not as vibrant as the inland hills, but the soft, muted colors of a salt marsh can be breathtaking. Rhode Island's coastline is often bypassed during fall foliage, but it has its own special beauty. Even if you miss the peak, or can visit only a single tree in a field, be sure not to overlook this fairest of all nature's displays.

For many – ourselves included – autumn brings a sense of urgency for one's need to be outdoors, to smell the woods, to feel the sun and to walk and ramble just a bit farther. There are times, such as on a clear, sun-drenched afternoon or cool morning, when wisps of fog rise to reveal the trees and then the beauty of the colors is hard to believe.

# A Few Tips

- ✤ Make reservations for lodging, or you might be sleeping in your car!
- ✤ While early October is the most popular time for a foliage ramble, consider September. Days are usually clear, warm and dry and the main roads are less crowded.
- ✤ Pack a picnic.

* Bring a camera and binoculars (good hawk-watching season).

* Consider purchasing a field guide to trees and wild-flowers. It always helps to know the name of beauty.

* Remember to respect private property, not litter and be courteous to other drivers, if necessary pulling over to let them pass. This is especially important during foliage season on narrow country roads. Remember, not everyone is on vacation when you are.

Although the routes described herein were chosen for their autumn appeal, most of them, quite naturally, are great trips any time of year, as each season has its own beauty. Many of the routes offer great swimming, boating, camping, hiking and skiing possibilities. Certainly, don't limit yourself to autumn – but don't pass it up either!

# Peepers' Hot Lines

| | |
|---|---|
| Connecticut Tourist Bureau | ☎ 800-282-6863 |
| Maine Tourist Bureau | ☎ 800-533-9595 |
| Massachusetts Tourist Bureau | |
| (foliage hot line) | ☎ 800-632-8038 |
| (seasonal hotline) | ☎ 800-227-MASS |
| New Hampshire Tourist Bureau | ☎ 800-258-3608 |
| | or 800-262-6660 |
| Rhode Island Tourist Bureau | ☎ 800-556-2484 |
| Vermont Tourist Bureau | ☎ 802-828-3239 |

*What a beautiful month October is! It is the opal month
of the year. It is the month of glory, of ripeness. I love to
think that when the summer, with all its fullness
of innate beauty, has gone through its course and is about
to die, it knows how to break out with more gorgeous
beauty and die with more glory on its head than it has in its
positive freshness and vernal beauty.*
Harriet Beecher Stowe

*I have been treading on leaves all day*
*until I am autumn-tired.*
*God knows all the color and form of leaves*
*I have trodden on and mired.*
*Perhaps I have put forth too much strength*
*and been too fierce from fear.*
*I have safely trodden underfoot*
*the leaves of another year.*
Robert Frost

*How beautiful when a whole tree is like one great
scarlet fruit full of ripe juices, every leaf,
from lowest limb to topmost spire, all aglow,
especially if you look toward the sun! What more
remarkable object can there be in the landscape?*
Henry David Thoreau

# Chapter 1

# Connecticut

# The Quiet Corner

SOUTHBRIDGE

84

MASSACHUSETTS
CONNECTICUT

191 131

WOODSTOCK

169

171

S. WOODSTOCK

44

POMFRET

44 101

N

6 BROOKLYN

169 395

14

CANTERBURY

# The Quiet Corner, Northeast Connecticut

 This ramble begins in Canterbury on Route 169 and heads north. From Route 395, exit onto Route 14 and go west to Route 169. Peak colors are from mid-to late October.

> **Highlights:** *Hayrides, hilltop views, quiet villages, Prudence Crandall Museum, Roseland Cottage, Old Trinity Church, pumpkin picking, a wolf's den, nature trails, Golden Lamb at Hillandale Farm, art museums, apple orchards, Brayton Gristmill and more.*

Route 169 is as scenic a back road as you will find in southern New England and it is an easy drive from the New York City area or from southeast Connecticut. Rolling hills, village greens, woodland trails and a diverse assortment of historic sites await your discovery. Some truly first-class inns, restaurants and shops are in this pocket of Connecticut called "The Quiet Corner."

## Canterbury

One of the best spots for enjoying autumn's color is right in the center of Canterbury, where maple trees are scattered about the First Congregational Church. Sitting atop a rise of land, the classic white church looks over a sloping green to the front and to its rear is a tiny library (once a one-room school). Across the street is the **Prudence Crandall House Museum**, a Federal-style house built in 1805. With twin chimneys, an elaborate entrance doorway and a Palladian window on the second floor, the house is a notable example of the Canterbury style of architecture.

In 1833, Prudence Crandall opened New England's first school for black females. For her act of courage, Miss Crandall was arrested and convicted of breaking a law that forbade the educational instruction of "colored persons who are not inhabitants of the state." Although freed on a technicality, a mob attacked the school and forced Crandall to shut down the academy.

Today, the home is a museum that chronicles the life of Prudence Crandall, black women's history and local history. There are also three period rooms, a gift shop and a small research library. Now a National Historic Landmark, the museum is open from Wednesday through Sunday from 10 a.m. to 4:30 p.m. Another way to enjoy Canterbury and the surrounding towns is to become involved in the "Walking Weekend," held in early October, when tours are given of historic greens, natural areas and mill villages.

Nearby, on Creasey Road, is **Wright's Mill Tree Farm**, where you can pick your own pumpkins, visit the farm museum or take a hay ride. The 250-acre farm is especially scenic with views, ponds and mill sites. Special events in the fall include an antique and craft show, spooky hayride and a haunted house. The children will enjoy the petting zoo and the lectures on landscaping and farm history will entertain the adults. Call ahead to see what's happening when you're in the area.

# Brooklyn

Driving north on Route 169, you will pass a combination of farms, residential homes and views of the rolling hills. Brooklyn has an especially attractive green with a statue of Revolutionary War General Israel Putnam atop a horse. Putnam was the colorful general who commanded the Patriots at Bunker Hill and his remains were reinterred at the base of the statue. The inscription on the equestrian statue reads, "Passenger, if thou art a soldier drop a tear over the dust of a Hero, who, ever attentive to the lives and happiness of his men, dared to lead where any dared to follow." The green is surrounded by handsome old buildings, some in the Greek Revival style and some in the Federal style. On Church Street is the **Putnam Elms**, a 1784 home that has been in the Putnam family for two hundred years and is open for tours on Wednesdays and Sundays (Brooklyn holds an October Fest with international food, music and dance in the early part of the month).

One of the most interesting sites in the area is **Old Trinity Church**, the oldest Episcopal Church in Connecticut, built in 1771. Just follow Route 6 east for 1.3 miles, then turn left onto Church Street. The church will be on your right. On my visit, I felt two distinct moods from the secluded setting. The church is surrounded by tall trees and old gravestones and, when I first arrived, clouds blocked the sun and the scene was a forboding one, full of dark shadows. Moments later, when the sun broke through, the entire atmosphere transformed. The trees that had added to the gloom were now ablaze with splashes of color and the white church looked beautiful in its simplicity. I found myself taking picture after picture and then wandered across the street to get a shot of the corn field that stretched back toward the western hills.

Another "must see," and hopefully "must eat," is the **Golden Lamb** at Hillandale Farm. This is one of the finest restaurants in Connecticut – certainly the most romantic – and dinner is by reservation only; it is usually booked months in advance. An evening meal at the Golden Lamb is more than just fine dining – it's an experience to treasure. Bob and Jimmie Booth have been running the restaurant for 31 years and know that a warm, convivial atmosphere and terrific food are an unbeatable combination. The cozy restaurant is in a restored 19th-century barn complete with fireplace and unusual antiques – check out the 1953 Jaguar roadster. In the warm-weather months, hayrides are offered and cocktails are served on a deck overlooking fields where horses graze. Dinner entrées of lamb, duck, chateaubriand and salmon are to be slowly savored. Dinner is offered only on Friday and Saturday, lunch is served à la carte Tuesday through Saturday.

If you're traveling with young children, I'd save dinner at the Golden Lamb for another time, but you should go there just to admire the scenery. The restaurant and farm are located on Bush Hill Road, just off of Route 169 a bit north of Brooklyn. This is one of my favorite roads in all Connecticut, lined by old fieldstone walls and huge maples that will make you feel as though you're in Vermont. The pastoral scenes, with sweeping meadows and rust-colored hills, are perfect for landscape photography. And, if you are a bicycle enthusiast, the back roads in this vicinity are generally quiet, with no steep hills.

Back on Route 169 heading north, you will see the **New England Center for Contemporary Art** with work from around the world displayed in a four-story barn and sculpture garden. Another point of interest is **Lapsley Orchards**, which is a perfect place for children. Kids will love to walk the fields, using poles to pick apples, or to take a horse-drawn hayride. It's a colorful place with produce sold from the barn and hundreds of pumpkins stacked out front.

# Pomfret

When you reach the junction of Route 101 in Pomfret, turn left on Route 101 and follow it for about half a mile to Wolf Den Drive on your left. This road will lead into Mashamoquet Brook State Park. The road is rough in spots, but the woodland of oak and maple, with an understory of mountain laurel, is worth the effort. Although maples are known for their dazzling color, I like the oaks for the subtle color changes they offer in autumn. The white oaks' leaves begin the season with a touch of yellowish gold, then turn tan and finally settle into a rich rust-brown hue before floating away on the breezes of late October and

November. (White oak is the state tree of Connecticut.) Red oaks have scarlet leaves and the two varieties can be told apart by closely examining the edge of their leaves. The red oaks have pointed edges and white oak leaves are rounded. The acorns of the oak are important food for wild turkeys, squirrels and other animals. Another reason I like this Pomfret back road into the park is because it leads directly to the path closest to the **Putnam Wolf Den**. Just follow the road past the camping area and look for the Wolf Den parking area on the left. There are picnic tables here. On my last trip, I stopped for lunch and listened to the unmistakable drumming of a ruffed grouse, a drum-roll sound that starts slowly and then picks up speed. I also took the time to read the story of how Israel Putnam in 1742 (recall the statue of this Revolutionary War general at Brooklyn) killed the last wolf in Connecticut here. After the wolf killed some of his sheep, Putnam tracked the animal through the snow for miles to its den located here. First he tried to smoke the wolf out of its rock tunnel, then he sent in his dogs. When both plans failed, Putnam – showing the courage that would make him famous in the Revolution – entered the den with a torch and musket and shot the wolf.

The story fueled my interest. I had to see the den and set off down the path. Brown leaves drifted down like snow and the woods had that wonderful scent which comes only in autumn. As I walked down the rocky path and through the boulder-strewn woods, it looked as if wolves could live here still. I was so enjoying the walk that I went right by the wolf den and the plaque that tells the tale of Putnam. Autumn walks have a way of leading you away from your intended destination, and I had the pleasure of walking for 30 minutes over these hills and hollows before I turned back.

The Wolf Den is actually only about 10 minutes from the parking area (it's on the right at a point where the path turns a bit to the left, making it easy to miss). The den is a small dark tunnel leading back into bedrock. The plaque in front dramatically describes Putnam's entrance into the cave: "And by the light of her angry eyes he shot and killed the marauder."

There are other points of interest at the park, such as **Indian Chair**, a natural stone formation in the shape of a chair that rests on a cliff offering nice views. A round-trip walk from the Wolf Den parking lot to the den and then to the Indian Chair is about 1½ miles in length. Although the terrain is hilly and you must pick your way around rocks, the trip is not especially difficult and there are plenty of places to stop and enjoy the autumn colors. Keep an eye out for witchhazel, a fall-flowering tree that pops its seeds out of furry capsules. The seeds can be propelled for up to 25 feet!

You should also check out the main entrance to the park on Route 44, because that is the site of the wonderful old **Brayton Grist Mill**. Used as a corn and grist mill, the equipment for operating the mill is still in place. Also inside are three generations of blacksmithing tools. The mill is open through September, but even if you arrive later, it's worth visiting this peaceful spot. Behind the mill, a small streams cascades over little rock ledges, making for a great photograph. If you enjoy outdoor photography, try standing on the bridge of Route 44 and shoot the scene looking downstream toward the mill. I have a lovely shot of the red mill above the stream with golden foliage framing the scene.

Although Mashamoquet Brook State Park will draw you off Route 169, the center of Pomfret will bring you back. It's a lovely town, with a traditional white church and ivy-covered brick buildings at the Pomfret School. The stone Christ Church, built in 1882, is another handsome building, with stained glass Tiffany windows. At the Vanilla Bean Café, you can stop for a casual lunch of top-notch sandwiches and salads.

# Woodstock

The final leg of our ramble continues north on Route 169 into Woodstock. First you will pass picturesque Spruce Hill Farm and the Woodstock Fair Grounds, where the annual fair is always held on Labor Day weekend. **Fox Hunt Farms Gourmet Shop** will be on your left, featuring 20 varieties of coffee, plus croissants, fudge, sandwiches, 50 cheeses and more.

Farther up the road is **Roseland Cottage**, a restored 1846 Gothic Revival mansion that looks something like a pink gingerbread house. Built by merchant and publisher Henry Chandler Bowen as a summer residence, he called the home his "painted lady" and surrounded it with rose gardens. Tours include the house, with its original furnishings, an indoor bowling alley in the barn, an ice house and an aviary.

Roseland Cottage overlooks the attractive town common of Woodstock, with large maples lining the edge of the green and a baseball diamond situated at its northern end near the Woodstock Academy. The town has preserved its character, carefully protecting the village green with its old burying ground, early meeting house and surrounding homes dating back to 1776. There are even a couple of old red barns within sight that serve as a reminder of New England's agricultural past. Just north of the town's center is **The Christmas Barn**, a unique shop in a red barn that carries collectibles ranging from quilts to country furniture.

The **Inn at Woodstock Hill**, once a privately owned estate situated on a hilltop, is both elegant and romantic with 22 suites and guestrooms. The rooms are decorated in floral chintz fabrics and have private baths, television and air conditioning. Six of the rooms have fireplaces. You could spend a weekend here and simply enjoy the area by foot, strolling through orchards, meadows and hills, soaking up the scenes of autumn in Connecticut's Quiet Corner.

# For More Information
*(Area code 860 unless noted otherwise)*

| | |
|---|---|
| The Christmas Barn | ☎ 928-7652 |
| Connecticut's Quiet Corner Tourist Dept. | ☎ 928-1228 |
| Connecticut Tourism Office | ☎ 1-800-CT-BOUND |
| Fox Hunt Farms Gourmet Shop | ☎ 928-0714 |
| Golden Lamb Buttery | ☎ 774-4423 |
| Lapsley Orchards | ☎ 928-9186 |
| New England Center for Contemporary Art | ☎ 774-8899 |
| Prudence Crandall Museum | ☎ 546-9916 |
| Roseland Cottage | ☎ 928-4074 |
| Walking Weekend | ☎ 928-1228 |
| Wright's Mill Tree Farm | ☎ 774-1455 |

# For Accommodations
*(Area code 203)*

**In Brooklyn**

| | |
|---|---|
| Barrett Hill Farm | ☎ 779-2686 |
| Tannerbrook | ☎ 774-4822 |
| American Family Inn | ☎ 774-9644 |

**In Pomfret**

| | |
|---|---|
| Clark Cottage at Wintergreen | ☎ 928-5741 |
| Cobblesoft | ☎ 928-5560 |
| Grosvenor Place | ☎ 928-4633 |
| Quail Run | ☎ 928-6907 |
| Baker Hollow Farm | ☎ 928-4423 |
| Hillside Bed and Breakfast | ☎ 974-3361 |
| Karinn | ☎ 928-5492 |

**In Woodstock**

| | |
|---|---|
| Ebenezer Stoddard House | ☎ 974-2552 |
| Beaver Pond Bed & Breakfast | ☎ 974-3312 |
| English Neighborhood Bed & Breakfast | ☎ 928-6959 |
| The Inn at Woodstock Hill | ☎ 928-0528 |

# The Litchfield Hills, Northwest Connecticut

 To get to Litchfield from Route 8, take Route 118 west. Peak colors are from mid- to late October.

**Highlights:** *Mountain-top views, estates, gardens, wineries, hayrides, fairs, historic sites, waterfalls, covered bridges, hiking, pick-your-own pumpkins, Housatonic River, old books, antique shops, trout fishing and more.*

Having traveled most of Connecticut, I'm convinced that the two most scenic sections are the northern corners of the state. The northwest corner, known as the Litchfield Hills, has the great combination of accessible mountain tops, hidden villages and the beautiful Housatonic River. Perhaps best of all, if you miss the peak colors of northern New England, the Litchfield Hills are still waiting for your arrival. Sometimes, autumn's show extends all the way to the first of November.

## Litchfield

Heading west on Route 118 into Litchfield, there are two interesting places to see before reaching the center of town. The first is **Topsmead State Forest**, located off Buell Road. It's a wonderful area for autumn colors, with open fields, views of surrounding hills and wildflowers. The property was the former estate of Miss Edith Morton Chase who, in 1925, had an English Tudor-style house built on the crest of a hill. Guided tours of her home are available on the second and fourth weekends of October. The outside of the house is as handsome as the inside.

It features a slate roof, brick and stucco walls, cypress woodwork and lead downspouts. Holly, lilac, juniper and a formal garden encircle the residence. You can stroll down a winding lane lined with apple trees or explore a seven-tenths-of-a-mile nature trail, which has interpretive signs.

## The Litchfield Hills

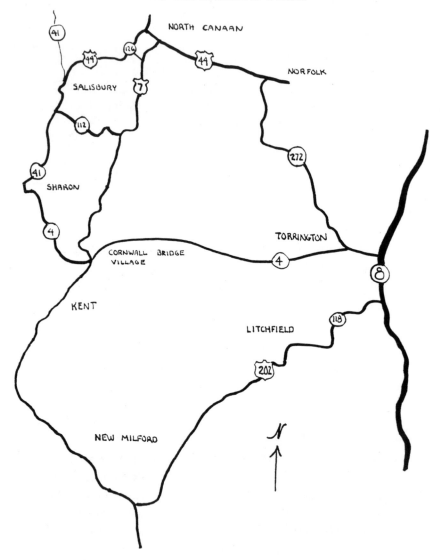

Nearby, on Chestnut Hill Road (off Route 118 just before entering Litchfield Center), is the **Haight Vineyard**. Established in 1978, this was the first farm winery in Connecticut, growing such grape varieties as Chardonnay, Riesling, Seyval Blanc and Marechal Foch. The vineyard is located on a hillside high above the Bantam River – you can't miss the giant wine barrel out front. Free tastings and tours are offered.

When you cruise down into the center of Litchfield, you might be surprised at how well preserved the picturesque town is, despite being so close to Hartford. In many respects, the town reminds me of Woodstock, Vermont, with its stately homes, small shops and wide assortment of cafés and restaurants. The town's common was laid out in the 1770s and it's a great place to stroll while admiring the old buildings, such as the courthouse made from granite blocks and the Congregational Church with its ornate steeple. If it's cold out, stop in at the Litchfield Food Company and warm yourself with a great cup of coffee.

If you enjoy bicycling, check out the back roads, such as Buell Road, before leaving the area, for relatively quiet rides through beautiful countryside.

Route 63 heading south from town is a scenic road, lined with old farms and wooded views. It will lead you to **White Flower Farm**, about three miles south of the center of Litchfield. The color at the farm can be breathtaking, with flaming orange sugar maples towering over hardy purple, white, red and yellow mums. Lichen-covered stone walls, grand old beech trees, weeping crab apples and perennials are just some of the flora you will see as you stroll through the display gardens. A knowledgeable staff in the retail store can help you pick out the plants with colors that catch your fancy.

Just west of the center of Litchfield, take a spin up Milton Road, which will be on your right as you head down Route 202. **Bunnell Farm**, at the corner of Milton Road and Maple Street, is a great place to stop in autumn, especially if you are traveling with children. Here, you can pick your own pumpkins, take a horse-drawn or tractor-driven hayride to the pumpkin patch or visit the farm animals. Inside the barn you can buy cider, apples, gourds and fresh produce.

Instead of heading back to Route 202 via Milton Road, try Maple Street, yet another scenic road, good for getting "lost" on and also great for biking. When you reach Route 202, you might want to turn left and visit the **White Memorial Conservation Center**, which has a fascinating natural history museum. (Just go back toward Litchfield a short distance and look for the signs.) With over 4,000 acres of forest, field, swamps and ponds protected, the grounds here provide a great way to get some exercise and learn about the natural world. There are miles of trails, one of which is the **Trail of the Senses**, where interpretive plaques suggest you use your senses – smelling the delicate fragrance of a flower or feeling the textures of lichens and mosses. There is also a self-guiding nature trail that passes glacial erratics, 200-year-old pines and a wide diversity of ground covers and wildflowers.

# Bantam Village

Our loop of the region continues by heading south on Route 202 and traveling through Bantam Village, where a number of antique shops will beckon you to stop. A short distance farther is **Mount Tom Tower and Pond**. If you plan on picnicking, the area by the pond is a great place to stop; or if you're in the mood for a little climbing, a one-mile loop trail leads to a stone tower atop the mountain. Although the distance is only a mile, it's a bit challenging as you gain 400 feet in just half a mile. The summit is at 1,291 feet and the view is worth the climb. You will see Connecticut's highest mountain, Bear Mountain, to the northwest and Everett Mountain in Massachusetts.

# New Preston

If you're looking for a less conventional view, proceed south on Route 202 into New Preston. At the traffic light, turn left, then bear right, circling behind a graveyard. I love the narrow, northward view through an opening in the trees that looks out on a nearby hill. Rising up from the golden-brown oaks, the dark green of pines and the orange foliage of maples is a white church steeple. From this vantage point, it seems to grow right out of the forested hills with no nearby town!

On the other side of Route 202, be sure to drive up Route 45 for a wonderful ride around Lake Waramaug. Before you reach the lake, there is an interesting crossroads at the village of New Preston. A pharmacy, barber shop, pottery shop and antique store are clustered around a small stream and the Old Pavillion Hall. Stand on the bridge and look downstream at the rushing water swirling by the old stone foundations of the homes. It's one of those little spots that has somehow held onto its charm in a world that thinks bigger is better.

Follow Route 45 up to the east end of the lake and then turn left onto Lake Road, which hugs the northern end of Lake Waramaug. The road climbs a hill and with each rise in elevation, the scenery improves. There are some wonderful inns tucked away back here, such as The Inn at Lake Waramaug, Hopkins Inn and Boulder Inn. Be sure to stop at **Hopkins Winery**, where both vinifera and French-American hybrid grapes are grown. You can taste the wines or take a self-guided tour through the winery which is located in a renovated 19th-century barn. And if you follow Hopkins Road through the vineyard and then go left on Curtis Road, you are afforded some spectacular views of the lake below and the hills beyond. Rail fences and horses in the pastures make the scene picture-perfect.

Back on the lake-side road, continue west, passing into Kent and then to **Lake Waramaug State Park**. At this time of year, it's a peaceful spot and you will have to share the picnic area only with ducks and geese. Just past the park is a small marsh area where you might catch sight of a wood duck (they begin to migrate south at this time of year). The male wood duck's plumage matches the splender of the autumn leaves, with iridescent patterns of green, purple, yellow and red. In fact, the males even have touches of blue, about the only color not found in New England foliage!

When you reach Route 202, head south. Book lovers should keep an eye out for **Reid & Wright Antiquarian Book Center**, in a building with a wonderful ornate wooden door. It will be on your left. Just beyond the book center is **Park Lane Cider**, where you can purchase a jug of fresh cider to take with you on your journey. Also, watch for a sign for **The Silo Gallery**, where continuing exhibitions of arts and crafts by local and nationally renowned artists are featured.

# New Milford

When you come down the hill into New Milford, bear right at the signs for Kent. You will pass the center of town with a lively village green surrounded by stores and older homes, many in the Greek Revival style. Then cross the Housatonic River, following Route 7 north.

It's hard not to love the Housatonic, named by Mahican Indians meaning "the place beyond the mountains." In some respects, the river is a place beyond our world – just sit on its bank and let the water hypnotize you with its power. An author from an earlier time, Chard Powers Smith, had similar feelings when he penned these words in his book *The Housatonic*: "The value of a river as a symbol of eternal truth is increased if the valley through which it flows likewise suggests permanence behind change, if the hills are wide and gracious under the sky...." Here in the Litchfield Hills, there is a sense of permanence and grace.

# Kent

The Housatonic rises from the Berkshires in Pittsfield and winds its way south into the Litchfield Hills, adding scenes of beauty around every turn. By following Route 7, one can see the very best of the river. In Kent, Bulls Covered Bridge graces the Housatonic, spanning a rocky section of riverbed below. On the west side of the bridge is a recreational area. If you are a photography buff, try following the riverside trail upstream for a hundred feet to capture the scene on film. Even without a camera, the worn rocks and potholes on the riverbed are worth the walk.

The center of Kent along **Main Street** (Route 7) is quite attractive, with handsome homes and tall maples. Some of the side streets, such as Maple Street and Railroad Street, are also worth exploring and it's best to park the car and spend a couple hours knocking about on foot. You can visit art galleries, restaurants, bakeries, upscale clothing stores and antique shops. If you're here during the beginning of October, inquire about the annual **Harvest Fair**.

One of the most fascinating stops on the entire ramble is the **Sloane Stanley Museum**, where a collection of early-American tools and implements tell the story of our ancestors' working life. The tools were donated by Eric Sloane, the writer and artist, who had a love of both history and craftsmanship. Sloane also discovered a small wood-backed, leather-bound diary from 1802 which is on display at the museum. Written by Noah Blake, the diary was incorporated into a book arranged by Sloane that features detailed pen-and-ink drawings of life on the Blake farm. I purchased the book at the museum and found it gave an incredible glimpse into a bygone way of life. Sloane's drawings revealed not only the way folks lived at the turn of the 19th century, but how things worked, how tools were used and the ingenuity of the settlers. Together, Sloane and Noah Blake give a history lesson that is pure pleasure to read.

Also on the property is a reproduction of the cabin young Noah Blake describes in his diary. Sloane built this too, and it includes an open stone fireplace and oven, table and chairs and unique log steps leading up to a loft. To the rear of the museum are the remains of the Kent Iron Furnace, built with granite blocks in 1826.

Just north of the museum along Route 7 is **Kent Falls**. From a distance, it appears the mountain stream drops off the edge of a cliff and tumbles 250 feet straight down. But if you climb up the adjacent trail, you will see that from a closer perspective the falls are comprised of numerous smaller drops, each with its own little pool.

The ride north on Route 7 seems to get more beautiful with each passing mile. On my last trip the setting sun lit golden rows of cornstalks and the mountains beyond, prompting me to seek out a high point of land to catch the sunset. At the village of Cornwall Bridge, I turned right onto Route 4 and wound my way up the hills to Mohawk State Forest. Driving to the top of the mountain, I was rewarded with views to the west and a sunset streaked with pink and even a bit purple.

One place you really must visit in the daytime is the center of **Cornwall Plain**, just off of Route 4. Quiet country lanes pass by two churches and front yards that still have hitching posts out front. But for me, the real attraction is poking around the back roads, such as Essex Hill Road and Valley Road. At one time this was the location of the Cathedral Pines, which was a rare stand of old-growth white pines. But a few years back, a tornado cut a swath through the outskirts of town, taking down everything in its path, including the pines. You can still see vivid reminders of the tornado's power in the broken trunks of enormous trees that stand on the hills like match sticks. It's wild country, where you are almost as likely to see beaver and deer as passing cars.

# Sharon

Another interesting side trip to take is toward Sharon, west on Route 4. On the way up, you will pass the **Northeast Audubon Center**, which has 11 miles of trails, herb and wildflower gardens, a bookstore and exhibits. The sanctuary's 684 acres are well suited to an autumn walk, featuring a pond, stream, marsh and forested hills. Beaver, osprey, otter and wild turkey are some of the wildlife you might see. Nearby is Ellsworth Hill Farm, which grows a dozen varieties of apples and produces apple cider.

The center of Sharon has a long narrow green laid out in 1739 and is one of the finest in all Connecticut. Well-preserved homes, some of them 18th-century brickwork, line the green. An unusual gray granite tower with a clock gives the town a character all its own. On my last visit, I stayed at a charming country home called the **1890 Colonial Bed & Breakfast**. Its main floor has fireplaces in the living room, dining room and den, while the guest rooms have high ceilings and private baths.

After visiting Sharon, be sure to return to Route 7 and go north to see one of the most beautiful covered bridges in New England. It's a long, red, one-lane bridge that leads to the little village of **West Cornwall**, home of Cadwell's Corner, where you can enjoy a hearty breakfast or lunch. Nearby is **The Cornwall Bridge Pottery Store**, featuring world-class stoneware and other fine craft work. **Jan Ingersoll Shaker Furniture Shop** is just down the road.

When I stopped to take pictures of the bridge, I couldn't help but wet a line in the Housatonic, an excellent trout stream. (Much of the river is designated as "catch and release" to help preserve the quality of the fishing.) Although I didn't catch anything, I had the pleasure of watching a great blue heron fly from a rock and wing its way upstream. These massive gray-colored birds stalk the edge of rivers, ponds and marsh, looking for minnows and frogs to snatch with their long bills.

# Salisbury

When you reach Falls Village at Canaan, just a few miles north of the covered bridge, take Route 126 north to Route 44 west into Salisbury. (Falls Village is home to **Riverrunning Expeditions**, who will outfit you to explore the Housatonic by paddle power.) Hills plunge down toward the river, signaling your entrance into more rugged country. Salisbury has a rich history and was called the "arsenal of the American Revolution" because of the many furnaces that manufactured metal here. Now, the forges and furnaces are quiet and the town has a wealthy charm, with large white homes surrounding a quiet green. In front of a unique-looking town hall is a stone pillar inscribed with a pointing hand and the words "to Bofton, 165 miles." Also there is a large stone kettle (1908) that serves as an outlet for fresh spring water. Local residents come here to fill jugs with the icy water. I met one gentlemen who still clearly recalls stopping here with a horse and wagon and giving the horse a good long drink from the kettle.

Salisbury is noted for its many antique dealers and tea companies. **Harney & Sons** supplies teas to the best hotels in the country and the Chaiwalla Tea Room serves exotic blends. On a cool autumn day, there is nothing quite like a good cup of hot tea.

There are some great hiking trails just outside of town and a nice mountain-top view is only a short walk from a back road. (The Appalachian Trail runs through Salisbury and you may have the good fortune to meet one of its intrepid hikers!) To reach Mount Riga, just turn onto Factory Road next to the town hall and follow it about three miles into the hills. Be warned that the road is steep, rough and turns from blacktop into gravel, so do not attempt this in inclement weather or near sundown. Where the road forks by a lake, stay to the right. You pass through a forest of hemlock, beech, oak and maple with an understory of mountain laurel, where chipmunks dash across the road and partridge burst into flight. During peak colors, part of this rugged lane resembles a tunnel carved through brilliant shades of yellows and oranges.

**Bald Peak** is about nine-tenths of a mile from where the road forks at the lake. There is a small shoulder to park on at the left-hand side of the road and a sign that says no camping. Mount Riga is privately owned land that is open to the public for walking – remember to "leave only footsteps and take only pictures." It's only a five- or 10-minute walk to Bald Peak, where a wonderful view awaits. On my walk, a couple from England was at the summit and commented on how I was the only hiker there on such a beautiful day. "You Americans don't do as much walking as we do." I said I was trying to change that!

There are more hiking trails at **Bear Mountain**, about a mile or two down the road. A sign marks the parking area and the hike to the Bear Mountain overlook takes about 45 minutes. Both mountain peaks are good spots for hawk-watching in September. Broad-winged hawks and other species ride the updrafts along the ridges as they migrate south, spiraling upward then peeling off toward their southern home.

# North Canaan

If you prefer not to give your car a workout, like the one it will get climbing Mount Riga, our ramble now heads to some more accessible hills to the northeast. Just follow Route 44 east out of Salisbury and into North Canaan, where you can stop for a bite to eat. Ice-cream lovers should check out the Whistle Stop Ice Cream Shop. For meals, try either the Depot Pub and Grub or Collin's Diner. Operating since 1941, Collin's Diner is a real old-fashioned road-side diner, small and homey and rated one of the top 10 diners in New England by *The New York Times*.

# East Canaan

Still following Route 44 to the east, we continue our loop of the Litchfield Hills. Along the way you cruise through East Canaan, where a small church sits off the main road in an open area with the mountains as a backdrop – yet another great picture! Even though we are leaving the Housatonic behind, the country is still beautiful, with numerous rolling hills offering incredible views. One of my favorites is from **Haystack Mountain** in neighboring **Norfolk**. (Where Route 44 intersects with Route 272, just follow Route 272 north a quarter-mile, look for the signs into the park and drive to the end of the access road.)

The first part of the hike up the mountain is a relatively easy 15-minute walk, followed by five or 10 minutes of vigorous climbing. When you reach the summit, you will wonder where the views are, but once you climb the stone tower, you can see in all directions. It's a superb place to soak up autumn's colors and, with a little luck, spot migrating birds circling above the hills. On my trip, I was mesmerized by a turkey vulture that soared directly above the tower, its wing span an astonishing six feet.

To complete the final leg of the loop, follow Route 272 south, passing through the tranquil center of Norfolk with a village green to rival Sharon's. For those who might not be able to hike but still want to be treated to a mountain-top view, **Dennis Hill State Park** (just south of Norfolk Center on Route 272) is the place to go. The entrance road alone is worth the trip, as it passes rows of maples shading gray stone walls. At the hilltop, a stone pavilion has stairs leading to an observation platform on its roof and the views are almost as good as Haystack's.

To return to Route 8 and 84, simply follow Route 272 south into Torrington and turn east on Route 4. Or, if you are completing the circle back to a night's lodging in Litchfield, you can go west on Route 4, then south on Route 63.

# For More Information
*(Area code 860)*

| | |
|---|---|
| Bunnell Farm | ☎ 567-9567 |
| Cornwall Bridge Pottery | ☎ 672-6545 |
| Haight Vineyard | ☎ 567-4045 |
| Harvey & Sons | ☎ 800-TEA-TIME |
| Hopkins Winery | ☎ 868-7954 |
| Jan Ingersoll Shaker Furniture | ☎ 672-6334 |
| Northeast Audubon Center | ☎ 364-0520 |
| Park Lane Center | ☎ 355-9213 |
| Reid & Wright Antiquarian Book Center | ☎ 868-7706 |
| Riverrunning Expeditions | ☎ 824-5579 |
| The Silo Gallery | ☎ 355-0300 |
| Sloane Stanley Museum | ☎ 566-3005 or 927-3849 |
| Topsmead State Forest | ☎ 567-5694 |
| White Flower Farm | ☎ 567-8789 |
| White Memorial Foundation | ☎ 567-0857 |

# For Accommodations
*(Area code 860 unless noted otherwise)*

**In Cornwall**

| | |
|---|---|
| The Cornwall Inn | ☎ 800-786-6884 |

**In Cornwall Bridge**

| | |
|---|---|
| Cornwall Inn | ☎ 800-333-3333 |
| Evie's Turning Point Farm | ☎ 868-7775 |
| Hitching Post Country Motel | ☎ 672-4880 |

**In Kent**

| | |
|---|---|
| Bromica Lodge | ☎ 927-3123 |
| Chauser House | ☎ 927-4858 |
| Club Getaway | ☎ 927-3664 |
| Constitution Oak Farm | ☎ 354-6495 |
| Fife & Drum Inn | ☎ 927-3509 |
| Flanders Arms | ☎ 927-3040 |
| Marvis Bed and Breakfast | ☎ 927-4334 |
| The Country Goose Bed & Breakfast | ☎ 927-4746 |

**In Litchfield**

| | |
|---|---|
| The Litchfield Inn | ☎ 567-4503 |

College Hill Farm        ☎ 672-6762
Tolgate Hill Inn        ☎ 800-445-3903

**In New Milford**

Heritage Inn of Litchfield County        ☎ 354-8883
Homestead Inn        ☎ 354-4080
Maple Leaf Motor Lodge        ☎ 350-2766
Rocky River Motel        ☎ 355-3208

**In Norfolk**

Blackberry River Inn        ☎ 542-5100
Greenwoods Gate        ☎ 542-5439
Manor House        ☎ 542-5690
Mountain View Inn        ☎ 542-6991
Weaver's House        ☎ 542-5108

**In New Preston**

Atha House        ☎ 355-7387
Boulders Inn        ☎ 868-0541
Country House        ☎ 868-1707
Hopkins Inn        ☎ 868-7295
The Inn at Lake Waramaug        ☎ 868-0563

**In Salisbury**

Ragamount Inn        ☎ 435-2372
The White Hart        ☎ 435-0030
Under Mountain Inn        ☎ 435-0242
Yesterday's Yankee Bed & Breakfast        ☎ 435-9539

**In Sharon**

1890 Colonial Bed and Breakfast        ☎ 364-0436
Sharon Motor Lodge        ☎ 364-0036

**In West Cornwall**

Hilltop Haven Bed and Breakfast        ☎ 672-6871

# Chapter Two

# Rhode Island

# The Hills of
# Southwestern Rhode Island

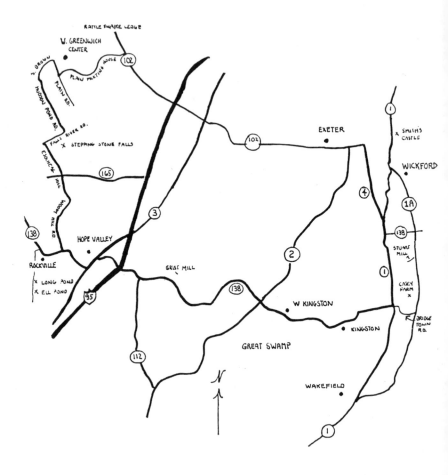

# The Hills of Southwestern Rhode Island to Narragansett Bay

 The first area to explore is around West Greenwich. From Interstate 95, take exit 5 to Route 102, then follow Route 102 north into this scenic town. Peak foliage is expected from mid- to late October.

> **Highlights:** *Rattlesnake Ledge, Stepping Stone Falls, Old Mill, hiking, Ell Pond, antiques, small farms, sweeping views, ospreys, Great Swamp, horseback riding, Historic Wickford, Silas Casey Farm, Gilbert Stuart House and Mill, Smith's Castle, coastal drive and more.*

I'll confess that I wondered if I'd find the country roads in Rhode Island that offered the autumn views and activities we discovered in the other states. On my fifth weekend of searching, I found what I was looking for in the southwest corner of the state. Here were vistas that were nothing short of spectacular, uncommon wildlife, cascading waterfalls and historic buildings that spoke of old New England. And because the state is so small, one can leave the explosion of foliage in the hills and explore the more subtle colors of the coast in a short drive.

# West Greenwich

When you exit Interstate 95, follow Route 102 about 3½ miles before turning left on Plain Meetinghouse Road in West Greenwich. Then go about three miles until you see a small parking area on the right at Rattlesnake Ledge, part of **Wickaboxet State Forest**. From here, it's only a 15-minute walk to a great view. When you follow the main trail into the woods, simply stay to the right at the fork and soon you will see the ledge on your left. From this vantage point, the forest rolls away to the south without a single sign of civilization. Red oaks shine a deep rust color set against a backdrop of dark green from the many white pines that grow in this rocky soil. Like most of New England, the trees here date back to the 1800s, when farmers abandoned their fields for better soil out west.

Only the whisper of breezes and the sound of chickadees, bluejays and white-breasted nuthatches greeted me on my trip. Later, a young couple, playing hooky from school, joined me on the ledge and told me about Ell Pond. "You won't think you're in Rhode Island when you see that place." They gave me directions and we sat at the summit for awhile talking about how warm it was for an October morning. I was reminded of Robert Frost's poem, "October":

> Oh hushed October morning mild,
> Thy leaves have ripened to the fall:
> Tomorrow's wind, if it be wild,
> Should waste them all.

The nooks and crannies in the granite ledge were once home to timber rattlers and thus the name of the hill. But the snakes, killed by the hundreds by locals who feared them, are today an endangered species in New England and it is illegal to kill one. In 30 years of hiking thousands of miles through the New England countryside, I have yet to see one of these large snakes.

There are many trails through Wickaboxet State Forest and I spent an hour following one to the west. I passed stands of cedar, sassafras with bright orange leaves shaped like mittens, low-bush blueberries with leaves flashing scarlet in the sun and aspen trees showing off vivid yellow foliage against a cobalt-blue sky. In addition to the white pine, small stands of pitch pine added the touches of dark green so necessary to bring out the best of the deciduous tree's color. (Colonists used the resin from these small, irregular-shaped trees on torches.)

As I was heading back to the parking lot, a goshawk gave an eerie cry, like that of a tree creaking in the wind. It stared at me for a few long seconds before taking wing and flying low through the woods, deftly navigating the many branches. Had this been spring, the bird may have made a pass at me – even dive-bombing my scalp – to scare me away from its nest.

Since the couple I met on the ledge talked so glowingly about **Ell Pond**, I decided to head in that direction, also noticing on my map that Stepping Stone Falls was on the way.

At the end of Plain Meetinghouse Road, there is a scene of bare-bones simplicity that symbolizes the very essence of New England's heritage. Built in 1750, the **West Greenwich Church** stands at a crossroads, looking something like a white one-room schoolhouse. Instead of the usual single entrance doorway to a church, this building has a window in the center of the front and a door on either side of that. Behind the church is the old burying ground. There is no traffic here, no other buildings nearby and with only the slightest bit of imagination, you can picture horse-drawn carriages bringing Sunday worshippers to church.

From the intersection of Plain Meetinghouse Road and Plain Road where the church sits, turn right onto Plain Road and follow that for half a mile and then turn left on Seth Brown Road. This quiet back lane has a small farm on it, but otherwise you pass only through oak woodlands. Seth Brown Road leads into Hudson Pond Road. In about two miles, take Falls River Road on your right. You will soon pass a small stream and tiny falls at what appears to be an old mill site. It's a tempting place to stop and you might want to wander around and do a little birding in the wetlands, but the more impressive falls are just down the road another quarter mile. These larger falls are called **Stepping Stone Falls** and they are absolutely beautiful. Swamp maples, flaming brilliant red, with a scattering of yellow-leafed beech trees, frame the blue pathway of the stream. Stepping Stone Falls is as accurate a name as there is. A series of small falls and pools twist over water-worn granite, inviting you to step down the rocky riverbed and explore this little paradise.

I stumbled upon the falls at peak color and immediately set up my camera to capture the beauty of the stream and trees. While snapping away, I made a mental note to return here with my brother Mark. He could spend a sunny morning here with his easel, while I went off in search of trout. I'm like the town crier – whenever I discover a special place, I can't keep it a secret. Having others experience the same reverence for beauty that I feel helps to not only protect the place itself but just might mobilize people to preserve other open spaces. You protect what you love.

# Exeter

If you continue on Falls River Road, up a steep hill, it will soon intersect with Escoheag Hill Road, where you should turn left. You will first pass an historic cemetery, then **Stepping Stone Ranch** (horseback riding, hayrides, country and Western shows) and the **Oak Embers Campground**, where all sorts of activities are geared for family campers. Just after you enter Exeter, you will meet Route 165. Exeter is home to the sprawling **Arcadia State Park**, where you can picnic or hike (entrance is just east on Route 165). Also in Exeter is **Our Kids Apple Farm** on Gardner Road, about seven or eight miles east on Route 165.

We continue toward Ell Pond by crossing Route 165 and proceeding south on Woody Hill Road. This country lane rolls through farms and woodlands where the shiny green leaves of mountain laurel twinkle in the understory beneath the reds, oranges and yellows of large trees. Drive slowly through this region, as you will probably have to share the road with horseback riders.

# Rockville

Soon you pass into the village of Moscow, part of the town of Hopkinton. You should then turn right (west) on Route 138, which leads into the village of Rockville. The handsome Baptist Church, on the left side of Route 138, sits far back off the road on a small hill surrounded by large maples and oaks. The next turn is a tricky one: take Wincheck Pond Road on your left, then again go left onto Canonchet Road. On the left, you will see the **Rockville Upper Mill**, built in 1844 and now simply called the Stone Mill, housing the village post office and some other town businesses. This massive stone block building was first a textile mill and then a rope mill. It has two lower stories of stone and an upper floor constructed of wood with rows of windows that allowed maximum natural light for the mill workers. It's truly one of the more handsome mill buildings in New England.

From the mill, it's a short drive to **Long and Ell Ponds Natural Area**. Simply follow Canonchet Road south a short way and then turn right onto North Road, passing Wichneck Pond. Look for a small parking area on the left (about a mile and a half from the mill). A rocky trail leads through thick growths of rhododendron and mountain laurel as it climbs the hillside. Soon, hemlock trees appear, giving one the feeling of being in northern New England. You will pick your way through shaded ledges, pass a tiny cave and go over a bridge of logs and after about 15 minutes, you'll reach the cliffs above the two ponds.

From here, you can go in several directions. All are worth exploring, but we take the left-hand trail to see the most spectacular view first. A five-minute walk brings you to a dramatic granite cliff that towers above Long Pond. Before I had seen this wonderful view, I would have thought this ramble in Rhode Island was best for those living south of here who could not make it up to the Berkshires or the mountains in northern New England. But this is such an enticing spot that folks like myself who live in Massachusetts should make a point of spending a day at Long Pond and Ell Pond. Because of its unique geological make-up, the area has been designated as a National Natural Landmark.

I spent a considerable length of time on this rock promenade. A turkey vulture was soaring over the pond and with each circular loop, it drifted a bit closer like a spirit on the breeze. Rusty-colored oaks mix with dark green pines on the opposite side of the pond's blue waters.

If you walk back to the intersection, there is another impressive view to the right that overlooks Ell Pond: a shallow L-shaped bog. And, from this main intersection, if you go straight downhill, you will descend into a gorge with solid stone walls on either side. The walk has been made easier by Appalachian Mountain Club members who have rearranged rocks to form a crude stairway. At the base of the gorge, a log bridge crosses a stream that separates the two ponds and then the trail angles to the left. Soon, you will be at an area known as "the cathedral," where massive hemlocks arch overhead and block out the sun. A few of the trees here are 200 years old, some of the oldest in all Rhode Island. It's the kind of place that makes you linger. Again I was reminded of a poem by Robert Frost that begins, "If tired of trees I seek again mankind." It may be a while before you trade the forests of Long Pond for mankind.

# Hope Valley & Kingston

To continue our ramble, make your way back to Route 138 and go eastward to where it connects with Route 3 at Hope Valley. This is a nice town to stroll around, checking out antique shops and having a bite to eat. At West's Bakery, you can have breakfast or lunch, but be sure to try their cream-filled pastry known as the Bismark. Across the street is the Hack and Livery General Store, a wonderful gift shop loaded with unique items.

In the nearby village of **Wyoming** you can explore the Wood River and take in fall's color from the vantage point of a canoe. For more than 20 years, Manny Point, of **Four Point Canoe Outfitters**, has been guiding canoeists on this scenic waterway.

**Meadowbrook Herb Garden** is another interesting place to stop and it's located just to the east of Hope Valley on Route 138. (You have to pass through a developed area along Route 138 in Richmond and then cross beneath Interstate 95.) There is a year-round greenhouse filled with over 250 varieties of herbs and perennials. The gift shop features herb seasonings, teas, spices, wind chimes, statuary, garden tools and wreaths.

# Richmond

At the junction of Route 112 and 138 in Richmond is the **Bell School House**, a one-room schoolhouse that is now the home of the Richmond Historical Society. You might want to explore more of the area by making a side trip south on Route 112 (there is an octagonal house on the left-hand side) and wandering the back roads through small villages of **Carolina**, **Shannock** and **Kenyon**. These towns were once humming with mill activity and signs of the past and even a few active mills can be seen along most waterways.

Our tour now heads toward the coast by continuing east on Route 138. On the way is **John and Cindy's Harvest Acre Farm** and produce market where you may want to stop and pick up some fresh fruits and vegetables. Right near the town line with South Kingston, you will enter the village of **Usquepaug**, where **Kenyon's Grist Mill** is located. Just turn left onto Old Usquepaug Road and then bear left on Glen Rock Road and you will arrive at the mill that was built the same year as the signing of the Declaration of Independence (1776). You're welcome to look around the tiny mill, still in operation, and walk out back to see the falls coming from the reservoir on Queens River and the old sluiceway that once brought the water to the mill.

Just a short distance east on Route 138 you pass the old Kingston Station on your right. Nature lovers may want to explore the **Great Swamp**, a broad area of wetlands that attracts all sorts of birds, including ospreys, wood ducks, herons, kestrels, red-tailed hawks and many others. To reach the swamp, simply turn right on Liberty Road and follow it until it ends at the railroad tracks and then go left on a gravel lane for about a mile to the parking area. A main trail heads into the swamp and leads to an open body of water. Remember to stay on the trail, as this is a wildlife-management area that is open to hunting.

Some of the more fascinating sites in the swamp are the many osprey nests the birds have constructed on top of the power-line poles that cross the center of the wetlands. Ospreys are fish-eating hawks with wingspans of 54 inches. They can be identified by the conspicuous crook in their wings. When hunting for fish, they sail over the water, then hover above the prey before plunging straight down to snatch a fish from the surface. Here at the Great Swamp, I was once treated to an aerial battle between two ospreys and a great horned owl that had taken possession of an osprey nest.

As you might expect, there is a heavy concentration of swamp maples here, which are among the first trees to turn color in the fall. Their red leaves make an interesting contrast with the shiny green leaves of the holly trees that grow in abundance along the trails leading to the water. The latter seem to catch the sun and twinkle on a clear day. The northern range of the holly is the southeast coast of Massachusetts and the holly trees here at the Great Swamp are among the largest I've seen.

Besides the many interesting natural features of the swamp, it is also a place of historical significance. During King Philip's War (1675-76), America's first major Indian War, the Narragansett

Indians inhabited the region around the Great Swamp. Even though the Narragansetts were neutral, the colonists, fearing the Narragansetts would soon enter the war, decided to stage a surprise attack on a winter encampment located deep within the swamp. On a bitterly cold and snowy winter's day, the soldiers, led by an Indian traitor, found the camp and massacred hundreds of Narragansett men, women and children. I became so fascinated by this war, I researched it for 10 years, which resulted in my novel, *Until I have No Country*.

# North Kingstown

Back on Route 138 our trip goes eastward, passing some fine old homes by the University of Rhode Island. Where Route 138 intersects with Route 1, cross Route 1 and follow Bridgetown Road to Route 1A, which hugs the coast of Narragansett Bay. One of the advantages of exploring Rhode Island's shoreline in autumn is the freedom from beach-going traffic. You can enjoy the golds and maroons of salt marshes and coastal vegetation at a leisurely pace.

By traveling north on Route 1A for a couple of miles into North Kingston, you will see a large white farmhouse set back on an open plain on your left. This is the historic **Silas Casey Farm**, dating back to 1750. Surrounded by stone walls, pastures and barns, the farm overlooks Narragansett Bay and Conanicut Island. It's such an attractive setting that it's impossible not to stop, even if just to snap a few pictures or walk the old road leading up to the farm. Three rooms are open to the public. They feature period pieces from over 200 years of the Casey family descendants. Survey equipment used by Thomas Lincoln Casey in the building of the Washington Monument and Library of Congress are on display. The dining room holds china from the 1700s, as well as documents, paintings and antique furniture. A reminder of the Revolutionary War is represented by a bullet hole in the parlor door, from an encounter between Patriots and British sailors from ships blockading Narragansett Bay. The Casey homestead is still a working farm. You can view the animals or walk down the old road in the back that leads to the overgrown Post Road; it once was a prominent north-south route.

An equally interesting historic site is the **Gilbert Stuart birthplace and Snuff Mill**. Just follow Route 1A north to Snuff Mill Road on the left and then continue on to Gilbert Stuart Road, where you bear left to reach the mill. Still in a rustic, wooded setting, the mill is worth a visit at any time of year, but it is especially beautiful in the fall when the surrounding beech trees splash the woods with yellow and orange. The scene is made complete by the red homestead and mill building, separated by a stream that tumbles out of the millpond.

Gilbert Stuart, the 18th-century portrait painter, was born here in 1755. He painted George Washington, John Quincy Adams, Thomas Jefferson and James Madison, among others. His unfinished oval portrait of Washington adorns the first U.S. postage stamp and the $1 bill. After you tour the home and mill site, be sure and walk along a pond-side trail that leads to an old burying ground beneath the beech trees. Benches at the water's edge invite you to rest and soak up the colors that reflect on the pond.

# Wickford

Returning back to Route 1A, follow it north into a town said to have more 18th-century buildings for its size than any other in New England. Wickford is a compact coastal village best explored by foot, the charm of the place energizing your steps. The town has its origins in fishing and trading and the old homes are fascinating in their diversity: Victorian, Federal, Georgian and Colonial houses line the narrow roads. At Saint Paul's Episcopal Church, dating back to 1874, pause to admire a three-story clock tower with an open arched belfry. Nearby, an even older church, the Old Narragansett Church (1707), is on Church Lane. It houses the oldest church organ still in use in America. Besides the history, Wickford is a shopper's dream, with a variety of small stores and art galleries.

An especially scenic spot is **Smith's Castle** on Smith Drive, north of town off Route 1. Just as we traveled northeastward from the Great Swamp, so too did the Colonial soldiers after attacking the Narragansett Indians. A marker at the Smith Castle reads: "Here were buried in one grave forty men who died in the Swamp Fight or on the return march to Richard Smith's Block House, December 1675." The original structure was burned shortly thereafter by the Indians, but owner Richard Smith rebuilt it using the old foundation and even some of the charred timbers.

It's a rather haunting spot, even in its beauty. The grounds overlook a small cove. Near the house, grape vines thicker than a man's thigh curl up the arbor. Adjacent to the castle is a replica of an 18th-century flower and herb garden. It is open for tours on fall weekends. If you stand quietly on the ancient pine boards, you just might hear echos of the past, as this is the only house left standing where Roger Williams, the founder of Rhode Island, is known to have lived and preached.

## For More Information
*(Area code 401 unless noted otherwise)*

| | |
|---|---|
| Arcadia State Park | ☎ 539-2356 |
| Four Point Canoe Outfitters | ☎ 359-7248 |
| John & Cindy's Harvest Acre Farm | ☎ 789-8752 |
| Gilbert Stuart Birthplace & Snuff Mill | ☎ 294-3001 |
| Meadowbrook Herb Garden | ☎ 539-7603 |
| Oak Embers Campground | ☎ 397-4042 |
| Our Kids Apple Farm | ☎ 294-9187 |
| Silas Casey Farm | ☎ 294-9182 |
| Smith's Castle | ☎ 294-3521 |

South Bristol County Tourism Council ☎ 800-548-4662
Stepping Stone Ranch ☎ 351-6312

# For Accommodations
*(Area code 401 unless noted otherwise)*

**In Hopkinton**
The General Thurston House ☎ 377-9049
Elizabeth McCuin ☎ 377-4975
**In Richmond**
Sun Valley Motel ☎ 539-8485
**In West Greenwich**
Best Western West Greenwich Inn ☎ 397-5494
Classic Motor Lodge ☎ 397-6280
Congress Inn ☎ 397-3381
The Stone Cottage ☎ 789-0039
**In Wickford-North Kingston**
The Narragansett House ☎ 294-3593
Bittersweet Farm ☎ 858-0053
Meadowland Bed and Breakfast ☎ 294-4168
The Moran's ☎ 294-3497
John Updike House ☎ 294-4905
Best Western ☎ 884-8000
Cove Motel ☎ 294-4888
Kingston Motel ☎ 884-1160
Oakside Motel ☎ 884-9153
Wickford Motor Inn ☎ 294-4852
**In Wyoming**
Cookie Jar Bed and Breakfast ☎ 800-767-4262

# Chapter 3

# Massachusetts

# The Hills of
# Central Massachusetts

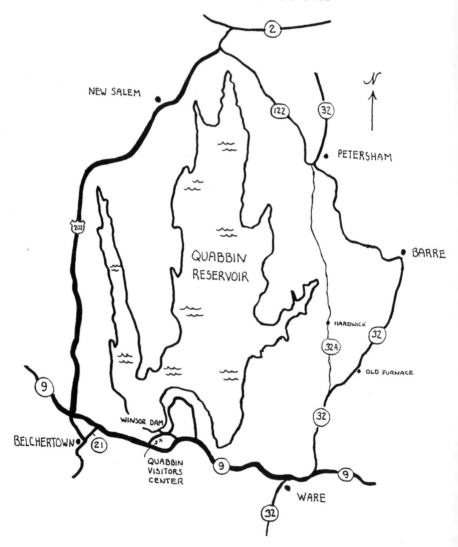

# The Hills of Central Massachusetts

 To reach the central part of the state from the Mass Pike, take the Palmer/Route 32 exit and follow Route 32 north to Route 9 west. If you're coming from the north on Route 2, exit onto Route 202 and you will pick up this ramble at the halfway point. Peak foliage is expected in mid-October.

> **Highlights:** *Quabbin Reservoir, Hamilton Orchards, Keystone Bridge, unusual rock formations, village greens, waterfalls, hilltops, Native American history, trout fishing, nature watching, historic structures and more.*

Slowly the quiet villages and the sprawling forests encircling **Quabbin Reservoir** are being discovered, yet the area still retains its charm. Back roads pass through orchards and wildlife reservations and over crystal-clear trout streams. There are no true mountains here, but plenty of easily accessible hilltops that afford panoramic views. And autumn is celebrated in country fashion in a number of towns with fall fairs, pumpkin contests and craft sales. Major cities such as Springfield, Hartford and Boston are all only an hour or two away.

Our route is a circular one, starting at the lower end of Quabbin Reservoir and looping around the region in a clockwise direction. A good way to start the trip is to get a look at the reservoir that helps make this area so special. Although four towns were "drowned" in the creation of Quabbin, the reservoir now helps to protect the integrity of the remaining towns by limiting development. Thousands of acres of forest have been left in their chusetts its drinking water. Quabbin itself is huge; over 38 square miles of water surface and 119 miles of shoreline.

# Ware

Great views of the reservoir can be seen from the Winsor Dam area off Route 9 in Ware. The islands you see far out in the water are actually the tops of hills that were flooded when the reservoir was created in 1939. The view here is always fantastic but especially so in the autumn when the blue of Quabbin is framed by rust-colored hills. Besides the Winsor Dam, there are several more lookouts nearby, such as the Goodnow Dike, the Enfield Lookout and Quabbin Summit Tower. Inside the visitors center, there are fascinating displays showing the creation of the reservoir and aerial photos taken before it was built. As we ramble around the reservoir, we'll visit a number of access points that are great for an autumn stroll with good chances of seeing some of the Quabbin's wildlife, including bald eagles, loons, coyotes, foxes and deer.

# Belchertown & Pelham

Belchertown is just a couple miles west on Route 9. Although the name is sure to cause a chuckle, the town center is really quite appealing. The village green is exceptionally long, with many maple trees and historic structures. If you are here in September, you won't want to miss the **Belchertown Annual Fair**. Just a few yards down Route 202 to the west is the Stone House Museum, which features artifacts and antiques from the town's historical association.

By following Route 202 north, you begin to circle the west side of Quabbin. Stop at **Pelham** to see the 1839 Congregational Church and the 1739 town hall, said to be the oldest one in continuous use in New England. Pelham was the home of Daniel

Shay, a Revolutionary War hero who led an uprising of farmers opposed to heavy taxation against the government in 1786. Behind the church is an interesting old burying ground with unusual headstones.

Waterfall lovers and those that enjoy walking along a mountain stream, should take the side road next to the town hall to **Buffam Falls Conservation Area**. Simply follow Amherst Road west 3.2 miles to North Valley Road (on your right), proceed six-tenths of a mile up North Valley Road and park at the pull-off on the left. Walk about 400 feet farther up North Valley Road and you will see an entrance sign to Buffam Falls. A path follows Buffam Brook through mountain laurel and towering hemlocks and in 10 minutes you will reach the falls where Buffam Brook converges with Amethyst Brook. The combination of sparkling water, yellow ferns, evergreens and a few red maples will have you reaching for your camera. Wild turkey are sometimes seen here, but not often as these birds can run and fly at fast speeds, unlike the domestic birds which are too fat to fly!

If you wish to extend your hike, there is a trail that follows Amethyst Brook upstream. Hemlocks are the dominant tree and you may notice that little vegetation grows beneath them. The hemlock needles are quite acidic and they blanket the ground, preventing other species from growing. However, porcupines have a taste for hemlock twigs and more than once I've seen one of these quilled woodland creatures far up in a hemlock, slowly munching away.

# New Salem

Continuing our loop around Quabbin, find your way back to Route 202 and proceed north, passing a scenic overlook of the reservoir on the right. As you travel into New Salem, keep your eyes peeled for a sign to **Hamilton Orchards**. The orchard is just a short way up West Road, which will be on your left. Here, you can pick your own apples or purchase cider, pie and other goodies in the store. Children, as well as adults, will love the place. There is a small petting zoo, swings and a nature trail. Watching a child's face when they pick their own apples is worth the trip.

I love to take autumn pictures here, always shooting the giant sugar-maple trees next to the farm house during the second week in October when they reach peak color. But even if the color isn't at its max, the pumpkins placed beneath the trees in large wooden boxes and the old-fashioned swing hanging from a branch are worthy of pictures.

I discovered that one of the best views of Quabbin was from the hilltop raspberry patch at Hamilton Orchards. Just walk past the farm house and turn onto the first dirt road on the right that leads uphill through apple and peach orchards and then through raspberries. Go all the way to the end of the road and then turn around. An incredible vista of the nearby hills is seen and Quabbin's deep blue waters sparkle in the distance. The hill is appropriately called **Serenity Hill** and it's the kind of place that invites you to rest and enjoy the scene.

From Hamilton Orchard, it's just a short drive north on Route 202 to my favorite village in the entire state – New Salem. A sign for New Salem will be on the right side of Route 202. When you reach the town green, you will have the feeling that time stopped. Twin spires from old churches rise up next to each other piercing the sky. An old burying ground, granite benches, hitching posts and traditional white painted homes add to the feeling that the town is locked in the 19th century. I have taken dozens of pictures here, but have yet to time my trip with peak color and bright sunshine. That gives me the excuse to keep coming back.

Book lovers should stop in at the **Common Reader**, a converted one-room schoolhouse on the green now serving as an antique shop and rare-book store. I love to browse the shelves, hoping to find a gem that others have overlooked. Near the bookstore is an old fire station with a ballfield behind it. An unmarked nature trail leads from here to a ridge that overlooks Quabbin. Thanks to the reservoir, the town has remained beautiful – the road gets little traffic as it abruptly ends at the reservoir forest.

On Route 202, opposite the entrance road to the village center, is the New Salem General Store and the Yankee Strudel Bakery. Pick up some goodies and have a picnic.

**North New Salem** is also a handsome section of town, located just a couple miles up Route 202 and then left on Elm Street. If you fall in love with this "west side of Quabbin," the place to stay is **Bullard Farm**, on Elm Street. Situated on the banks of the Middle Branch of the Swift River, this charming 200-year-old colonial home has been lovingly owned by the Bullard family for the past 120 years. I've enjoyed a few wonderful stays there, curling up with a good book by the fireplace in the Harvest Room. Conservation land surrounds the property and out back are high-bush blueberries, rhododendrons, azaleas and other plantings.

When Massachusetts Bay Colony was first settled, the coastal area and the valley along the Connecticut River were more attractive to the farmers than the wilds of central Massachusetts. In fact, much of central Massachusetts was controlled by the Nipmuck Indians well into the 1600s and only a few scattered settlements, such as Brookfield, were in the hands of the Puritans. When King Philip's War broke out in 1675, the Indians used central Massachusetts as a staging area from which to launch raids on English towns. It is said that the bloody raid on Deerfield was launched from an area of New Salem, now called the Bears Den, located off Elm Street on Neilson Road.

**Bears Den** is now owned by The Trustees of Reservation and has been preserved for all to enjoy. A five-minute walk from the parking area leads to a beautiful waterfall shaded by mighty hemlocks. Like most streams in Massachusetts, the Middle Branch of the Swift River, which tumbles through the property, was harnessed for its water power. Foundations of an early grist mill can still be seen here.

While the Bears Den offers natural beauty, the **Keystone Bridge** showcases man's craftsmanship. By following Route 202 to the north end of Quabbin and then turning south onto Route 122, you will arrive at Gate 30 on your right. The gates around Quabbin signify various access points into the reservoir and most are open to the public. By walking just a hundred feet down Gate 30, you reach the Keystone Bridge, which spans the Middle Branch of the Swift River. (Quabbin is fed by three branches of the Swift River.) Large stones fit neatly into place forming an arch over the rushing water below. The best way to view this small bridge is to walk down to the level of the river. On a clear day, looking through the arched tunnel of the bridge, sunlight dances on the river making it shine and sparkle on its way to fill the Quabbin.

Anglers may want to give the river a try for trout or fish the Quabbin itself. Boats can be rented at Gate 31, but you must have a Massachusetts fishing license. Smallmouth bass, lake trout, rainbow trout and salmon all cruise the depths of the reservoir. On my last outing, I caught only a small bass, but I had the pleasure of watching two bald eagles come and go from an island where they may have had a nest.

# Petersham

By following Route 122 south and turning on Route 32 for a short distance, you arrive at Petersham Center. With a number of Greek Revival buildings clustered around a village green, Petersham is quintessential New England. Try visiting the Country Store for lunch or a piece of pie and coffee and, if the weather is warm, carry it out to the gazebo.

Thoreau called October "the month for painted leaves" and at **North Common Meadow** autumn displays one of its finest scenes. Located just a hundred feet north of the Country Store on Route 32, North Common Meadow features a rich assortment of natural habitat. A meadow filled with wildflowers slopes down to a small pond that abuts heavily forested hills. Meadowlarks, bobolinks, kestrels and bluebirds all can be found in the open areas.

Before walking down the trail to the pond, take a moment to pause on Route 32 and soak up the scene beside the Brooks Law Office (1885). Old sugar maples rising next to the office add dazzling color in the foreground and beyond, the greens and yellow of the field blend into the muted rust-colored hills. Goldenrod and aster form patterns of yellow around the dark blue waters of the pond. It's an easy walk through the meadow and it's possible to loop behind the pond and return to your car via East Street. The forest adjacent to the meadow is part of the **Brooks Woodland Preserve**, a much larger property that has trails crisscrossing the East Branch of the Swift River. In contrast to North Common Meadow, Brooks Woodland has more rugged terrain with rocky outcrops, scattered boulders and dark woods of hemlock, hickory, birch and pine. Besides the access point from North Common Meadow, you can follow a riverside trail from Quaker Drive, about two miles south of Petersham off Route 122/32.

# Phillipston

If you happen to be in the area over the Columbus Day Weekend, be sure to visit Phillipston, where the **Giant Pumpkin Contest** is held annually on this holiday weekend. Phillipston has a tiny town center that looks as peaceful as can be. The half-circle village green is framed by a few buildings, most notably the **Congregational Church**, which dates back to 1785. I once went up to the steeple to see first-hand the wooden wheels of an ancient clock. It once used a 417-pound boulder as the pendulum. Phillipston is just to the northeast of Petersham; take Route 32 north to Route 101 east.

For a hilltop view, try the **Swift River Reservation**, about 2½ miles south of Petersham down Route 122/32, opposite the dam at Conners Pond. (The walk to the overlook takes about an hour and 15 minutes, round-trip, so leave well before dusk.) By following the trail that parallels the river in a downstream direction, you will enter a forest of old-growth pine and hemlock. Wildlife you might glimpse here includes beaver, weasel, porcupine, deer, fox, coyote, ruffed grouse, great horned owl and various hawks. Believe it or not, there are even a few moose in this part of Massachusetts and one was sighted at this reservation.

The trail ends along the river at a steel gate, but just before it is a footpath on your right that leads up a wooded hill. Follow that trail to the next intersection and turn left, followed by a quick right at marker #79. It's about a 10-minute walk to a rocky outcrop on your right, where a faint trail winds up the ledge to the overlook. The view is eastward, over Conners Pond, to the hills beyond. It's a wonderful, secluded place to rest and enjoy this special time of year. Descend the ridge by retracing your steps to marker #79 and then following the downhill path by the power line (instead of turning right onto the path you used to ascend).

The last leg of our trip follows Route 32 south all the way back to our starting point in Ware. On the way, you might want to check out the unusual "**Rockingstone**." It can be a bit tricky to find, but if you look for a right off Route 32 near the Petersham/Barre line, called Rockingstone Park Road, it will take you to this strange glacial configuration of boulders. One giant rock rests atop another and both are perched precariously on the granite ledge. Nearby, on Old Dana Road, is **Hartman's Herb Farm**, where over 250 varieties of herbs are grown. You are welcome to walk around the grounds of this little farm and visit the gift shop loaded with country crafts.

# West Brookfield

Our final stop is in West Brookfield, a few minutes ride south on Route 32. First you will pass through **Barre**, where there are a number of shops and restaurants. Route 32 intersects Route 9 farther south near the border of Ware and West Brookfield. When you reach this point, travel east on Route 9 for 1½ miles and look for the Rock House Reservation parking area on the left.

The **Rock House** is a 30-foot rock shelter used by Native Americans for thousands of years. The open end of the overhanging rock faces the southeast to catch the warming rays of the sun and the shelter looks something like a giant lean-to. In the winter, a five-foot section of ground beneath is always free of snow and ice. It's easy to use a little imagination and picture Indians huddled around a campfire, discussing an upcoming hunt.

A small pond lies directly in front of the shelter and the fall colors here are fantastic. Swamp maples turn a fiery crimson and the brilliance reflects off the water, mixing with the green of the conifers, the yellow of the beeches and the golden-brown tones of oaks. A small trail-side nature center sits on a hill overlooking the pond, making a fine stop for a picnic. From the Rock House, you can travel into West Brookfield, home of the renowned **Salem Cross Inn**, which features fine dining. There are many historic sites in town. For those interested in learning more about Greater Quabbin, a complete review is given in *Quiet Places of Massachusetts,* also by Hunter Publishing. To return to Ware and the Mass Pike, head west on Route 9.

# For More Information
### *(Area code 978 unless noted otherwise)*

| | |
|---|---|
| The Common Reader | ☎ 544-7039 |
| Hamilton Orchards | ☎ 544-6867 |
| Hartman's Herb Farm | ☎ 355-2015 |
| Phillipston Town Hall | ☎ 249-6820 |
| Quabbin Visitors Center | ☎ 413-323-7221 |
| Salem Cross Inn | ☎ 508-867-8337 |
| Swift River Reservation | ☎ 840-4446 |

# For Accommodations
## *(Area code 978 unless noted otherwise)*

**In Barre**
Harding Allen Estate B&B ☎ 355-4920
Hartman's Herb Farm Bed and Breakfast ☎ 355-2015
Stevens Farm Bed and Breakfast ☎ 355-2227
Jenkins House Bed and Breakfast Inn ☎ 355-6444
**In New Salem**
Bullard Farm ☎ 544-6959
**In Petersham**
Winterwood ☎ 724-8885
**In Ware**
The 1880 Inn ☎ 413-967-7847
Bed & Breakfast at Wildwood Inn ☎ 413-967-7798

# A Southern Berkshire Loop

 The Mass Pike will lead to Berkshire County, as will Routes 7 or 8 from the south. Peak foliage is expected from early to mid-October.

**Highlights:** *Tyringham Cobble, Gingerbread House, waterfalls, Chesterwood, historic Bidwell House, Colonel Ashley House, Bartholomew's Cobble, Monument Mountain, Berkshire Botanical Garden, Norman Rockwell Museum, Naumkeag House, antique and craft shops, small villages and more.*

It's surprising how many residents of eastern Massachusetts head north each autumn without ever having visited the **Berkshires**. Located in western Massachusetts, the Berkshire Hills extend from Vermont southward to the Connecticut border. The region below Stockbridge is especially scenic. The area offers a wide array of activities and there are many hidden places to explore. Having grown up in western Massachusetts, I have a special love for the Berkshire's many unique natural areas that represent the best of the great outdoors.

## Tyringham & Monterey

The ramble described here makes a large loop of the southern Berkshires, starting at the town of Lee, which has an exit off the Massachusetts Turnpike. From the exit, simply follow Route 102 south a few hundred feet and turn left onto Tyringham Road. Tyringham is one of those towns that has somehow balanced people with open space, where golden fields are framed by rolling hills ablaze in autumn's color. In fact, it was the rolling hills that center of Tyringham. The Gingerbread House is the nickname given to the Tyringham Art Galleries, where a diverse assortment of paintings and sculptures are exhibited. While the roof looks like it's made from thatch, it's actually comprised of several tons of shingles set in wavy lines to resemble mountains. Rock formations scattered out front add to the enchanting feel of this special place. Behind is a small sculpture garden and pond, while across the street is Sunset Farms, where maple products are sold.

## A Southern Berkshire Loop

The center of Tyringham has a simple white church sitting on a rise of land with a burying ground and fields behind it. As beautiful as this scene is from the ground, it's even better from **Tyringham Cobble**, a 400-foot hill from where there are sweeping views of this idyllic valley. To reach the path that leads up the hill, just follow Jerusalem Road three-tenths of a mile from the center of town and park at the small lot on the right.

The walk to the summit, first through pasture and then into woodlands, is not strenuous. Occasionally, there are openings in the foliage where you look down at a red barn below. You will pass a twisted rock formation that juts skyward, then the woods open to a hillside field. During September, this open area will be bright yellow with goldenrod, offset by the occasional splash of crimson from blueberry leaves and staghorn sumac. Staghorn sumac gets its name from its dense hairy stems and fruits which look like the velvet stage of a stag's antlers. It tends to grow in old fields and along sunny borders, while the poison sumac prefers shady conditions in swamps and low, moist areas. Joe-pye weed will also be blooming if you are here in the beginning of October. This is also a good time to spot migrating monarch butterflies as well as various birds, such as yellow-rumped warblers and large congregations of blackbirds. Having the good fortune of a sunny day, foliage at its peak and wildlife on the move can make memories that will warm you come winter.

Years ago, the upper slopes of the Cobble were farmed, but the rocky soil has since been reclaimed by the forest and a stately stand of white birch awaits you as you make your way to the summit. Its clear yellow leaves are beautiful, especially when your eye can take in both the white trunk and the foliage. There is one particularly handsome birch at the summit of the cobble which provides a great contrast when composing a photograph of the valley far below. Hawks, including broad-winged and sharp-shinned, are sometimes seen riding the thermals in autumn. It's pure pleasure to watch them and the best viewing time is usually mid-September on clear days.

The exposed rock ridge of the summit is thought to have broken off from nearby Backbone Mountain and flipped over eons ago. No matter how it was formed, this hilltop is a romantic spot and you shouldn't miss it – there is nothing quite like the top of a mountain and open sky above to make you feel alive. Total climb to top takes only about 45 minutes.

To continue our ramble, head south on Tyringham Road, but be sure to look back occasionally at the hill you just climbed. The scene past a split-rail fence and across a field toward the Cobble is another one to catch on film. When you reach the intersection with Monterey Road, turn right, then turn right again on Art School Road. If you enjoy finely crafted pottery, be sure to stop at **Joyous Spring Pottery**, which will be on the right side of the road. At the end of Art School Road is the historic **Bidwell House**, a Georgian saltbox constructed in 1750. The house is complemented by a wooded setting and gardens. With a little imagination, it's easy to feel as though you're back in another time. In the house are four fireplaces, two with beehive ovens, and large symmetrically placed rooms opening off the front stairwell.

After visiting the Bidwell House, proceed south on Monterey Road into the little village of **Monterey**, complete with an old-fashioned general store. For those who enjoy late-season camping, Beartown State Forest (off Blue Hill Road) has a number of sites, as does nearby **Sandisfield State Forest**.

At Monterey, go west (right) on Route 23. If you love waterfalls, there is a small but scenic one just off Route 23 on River Road, which will be on your left. There is something about white falling water passing through narrow channels canopied by vivid foliage overhead that makes me want to linger at such a spot and just listen.

# Great Barrington & Ashley Falls

Route 23 will carry you past Butternut Basin and into Great Barrington, one of the larger towns in the Berkshires. Here, you will find a number of shops, restaurants, inns and motels and the center of the town is compact enough to explore on foot. Just south of town, there are two very interesting areas to visit. The first one is in **Ashley Falls**, where The Trustees of Reservations, a nonprofit conservation organization, owns both a unique natural area along the Housatonic River and a historic homestead on a nearby back road. Follow Route 7 south to 7A south, then go right on Rannapo Road for about a mile and a half to Cooper Hill Road. The **Colonel Ashley House**, built in 1735, is on the National Register of Historic Places and is one of the oldest homes in Berkshire County. Like the Bidwell House, I love it because of the setting – on a quiet country road with plenty of open space around it. Tours are offered and you can see firsthand the fine craftsmanship, exemplified by the curved staircase and "sunburst" cupboard.

**Bartholomew's Cobble** is nearby on Weatogue Road and covers 270 acres along the Housatonic River. (The Housatonic offers some fine flat-water canoeing through woods and rich low-lying agricultural land.) Unusual rock formations, hundreds of plant species and great birding are just some of the reasons to visit Bartholomew's Cobble. Besides the woodland colors, there are open fields with their own special autumn hues from goldenrod and aster. The riverside trail is only a short walk from the parking area and is worth the trip. Giant white pines and hemlocks shade your way and ledges alongside the Housatonic offer sweeping views of the river and lowlands.

# South Egremont

The other area south of Great Barrington deserving of a visit is the town of South Egremont, a small peaceful village with a center that's so well preserved that it's a National Historic District. Penny candy still sells for a penny at the 150-year-old Gaslight Store and the entire town offers a trip back in time. **The Egremont Inn**, with porches upstairs and down, dates back to 1787 when it was a stagecoach stop. During the Civil War, the inn was used as both the town hall and a hospital. In the living room, you will see a curving brick hearth, once a blacksmith's forge.

Another great inn is the **Weathervane Inn**, which began as a farmhouse in 1785. During my stay there, I met fellow travelers having a drink around the fireplace and we traded tips on some of the more scenic spots in the area. **Bash Bish Falls**, in nearby **Mount Washington**, was on everyone's list and the next morning I set out to see the 80-foot falls myself. At the time, I didn't realize the best access to the falls was from Copake, NY, so I coaxed my ancient Subaru over some very rugged roads through Mount Washington. The trip was rough on the car, but there were a number of nice views and, once at the falls, I was glad I came. This beautiful but remote area of Massachusetts has few visitors and I felt as though I was in the White Mountains rather than the Berkshires. (Mount Washington has the fewest residents – under one hundred – of any town in the state!)

It's possible to form a loop of the southern Berkshires and return back to the Mass Pike by going north on Route 7 toward Stockbridge. One of the best places to capture the colors of the hills is from the summit of **Monument Mountain**. Hiking trails up the mountain branch out from a small parking area on Route 7, about halfway between the center of Great Barrington and Stockbridge. White birch, oak, striped maple and beech are just some of the trees that add their distinctive colors to the mountain's collage.

The direct route to the top takes about 45 minutes and it is a strenuous walk, but oh, what a view. Below are the hills, marshes and river valleys, with distant mountains stretching off to the west. Monument Mountain has had its share of famous visitors, including Hawthorne and Melville who first met here. William Cullen Bryant also came to the mountain and was so impressed he wrote a poem:

*Thou who wouldst see the lovely and the wild*
*mingled in harmony on Nature's face,*
*ascend our rocky mountains.*
*Let thy foot fail not with weariness,*
*for on their tops the beauty and the majesty of earth,*
*spread wide beneath, shall make thee to forget*
*the steep and toilsome way.*

# Stockbridge

After tackling the mountain, you deserve to treat yourself and Stockbridge is just the place for dinner or a drink. Home of the popular Red Lion Inn, Stockbridge serves as the hub of the area, with numerous shops, galleries and historic sites. It is also home of the **Norman Rockwell Museum**, where you can see art treasures by America's favorite illustrator. The museum is on Route 183, just north of Stockbridge. Nearby is another "must see": **Chesterwood**, the home, studio and garden of Daniel Chester French, sculptor of the Lincoln Monument in Washington, D.C. Also in Stockbridge is the **Berkshire Botanical Garden** (on Route 102 at the intersection with Route 183). This 15-acre garden features herbs, perennials, ponds and woodland trails. In October, the annual Harvest Festival is held here. My favorite spot in Stockbridge is **Naumkeag**, an estate built on the side of Prospect Hill. Naumkeag is a Native American word meaning "haven of peace," and that's exactly what you feel when you spend some time here. Joseph Choate bought the property in 1886 and had the 26-room "summer house" built, complete with gables, alcoves and porches designed to take maximum advantage of the views. The grounds are a wonderful place to stroll, with vistas, terraced gardens, a reflecting pool, a walled Chinese garden and a stand of white birches that offer vibrant hues for your autumn visit.

# For More Information
## *(Area code 413)*

| | |
|---|---|
| Berkshire Botanical Garden | ☎ 298-3926 |
| Bidwell House | ☎ 528-6988 |
| Colonel Ashley House | ☎ 229-8600 |
| Joyous Spring Pottery | ☎ 528-4115 |
| Norman Rockwell Museum | ☎ 298-3579 |
| Naumkeag | ☎ 298-3239 |
| Sandisfield State Forest | ☎ 258-4774 |
| Southern Berkshire Chamber of Commerce | ☎ 528-1510 |
| Tyringham Art Galleries (Gingerbread House) | ☎ 243-3260 |

# For Accommodations
## *(Area code 413)*

| | |
|---|---|
| Berkshire Visitors Bureau | ☎ 443-9186 |
| Egremont Inn, South Egremont | ☎ 528-2111 |
| Stockbridge Lodging Association | ☎ 298-5327 |
| Stockbridge Chamber of Commerce | ☎ 298-5200 |
| Southern Berkshire Lodging | ☎ 528-4006 |
| Weathervane Inn, Egremont | ☎ 528-9580 |

# Chapter 4

# Vermont

# Southern Vermont

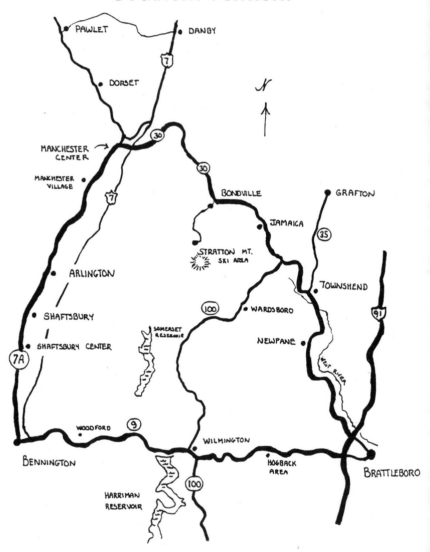

# *Southern Vermont*

 This trip begins in Brattleboro. Take Interstate 91 to Brattleboro and get off at exit 2. From there, the loop continues north on Route 30 to Manchester, south on Route 7A toward Bennington and then east on Route 9 back to Brattleboro. It can be done in two days, but more time is recommended. Peak foliage is expected between October 5th and 11th.

**Highlights:** *Beautiful river views, longest covered bridge, Stratton Mountain and resort, gondola rides, Mt. Equinox Skyline Drive, Hogback Mtn overlook, historical towns, major art exhibitions, excellent bookstores, Harriman Reservoir, Norman Rockwell Exhibition & Gift Shop, state parks, historic inns and taverns, fairs and festivals, superb foliage and more.*

An early Indian summer embraced the falling and rising southern Vermont hills which faded into a haze of orange, crimson and blue. The autumn aroma, bathed in the warmth of the day, was unmistakably familiar and intoxicating. If ever a day could cast a magical spell, this had to be it. In fact, my good fortune was sustained for the better part of three days as I traveled this area, exploring more roads than I can recall. Though I've chosen a rather large loop for this excursion, I know that the points of interest I mention only scratch the surface of all that this region has to offer. It is next to impossible to do the area justice, or the whole of Vermont for that matter, especially when it comes to its natural beauty. One can only hint at the wonders, both subtle and grand, of the Green Mountain State, whose mountains are anything but green come mid-October.

# Brattleboro

Brattleboro, a long-time favorite of mine as far as Vermont "cities" are concerned, is our starting point. There are three Brattleboro exits off Interstate 91, but exit 2 is probably the most direct route into the downtown area. There's plenty of metered parking to be found and if you haven't explored the town already, you're missing out – especially if you are a book lover. There are four or five good bookstores in the area where High Street intersects Main.

Take a walk down Main Street and visit the **Museum and Art Center** at historic Union Station at the corner of Main and Vernon. If you then become a little thirsty, the **Windham Brewery** on Flat Street is the place to go. Look for the **farmers' market** as well, on either Western Avenue or on the common, usually held on a Wednesday. If you come to town in late September, you may be lucky enough to catch the **Apple Days Festival**, also on the common. Call the Chamber of Commerce for exact dates.

Heading north on Main Street, bear left onto Linden Street (State Route 30) and in minutes you will find yourself well out of town following the wonderful West River. Since the river will be on your right, you will not only get the best views between Brattleboro and Newfane, but it will be easy to pull off the road. Watch for the large Black Mountain Antique Center on your right in **West Dummerston**.

You can't miss the long covered bridge spanning the river just beyond the antique center. It's closed to automobile traffic now, which is forgivable since it was built in 1872, but there is a good-sized parking area and you can get out and walk the bridge, catching some nice views from the triangular windows. I have a habit of measuring each bridge by my walking stride and this one turned out to be exactly one hundred steps. That's no small feat for an old covered bridge, though it's not the longest one in

Vermont! From here, the road begins a gradual climb uphill toward the town of Newfane.

# Newfane

The original Newfane Village was founded in 1774 two miles from today's site. But, wonders never ceasing, in 1825 a good part of the village was moved with the help of ox sleds to the flatter land. During the next 25 years, the newly relocated village was added to, thus creating the incredibly beautiful town you see today.

The first time one approaches the small village, there is an exciting sense of discovery, as if you alone have found it before the rest of the world. Such is the nature of many of these quiet Vermont hamlets. Look for the Moore Free Library on West Street and pick up the excellent brochure, which includes a map of the village and a brief history of each historic building.

Beyond the quiet dignity of the old building, there is a wonderful sense of space and design in the layout of the town. It is simple, yet never boring and always livable. Take some time to walk around and enjoy this gem of a town.

Along the road, just outside of town, I came across an unusual and amusing sight. A gray-haired old-timer, who at a glance looked well beyond the retirement years, was riding his antique bicycle down the road. It was the kind of bicycle found only in some yesteryear museum or in the circus perhaps, with an enormous front wheel as thin as a pencil and a tiny tag-a-long rear wheel, with the brave soul (or crazy fool) perched some seven or eight feet off the pavement. As I drove by, straining my neck to look up at him, he waved. Surely he knew what he was doing and perhaps it was even the same bike he rode as a youngster way back when. But the sight of him up in the stratosphere (without a helmet, mind you) was a bit sobering. And by the way, how does he stop?

# Townshend & Grafton

About five miles beyond Newfane on State Route 30, you will pass several more antique shops before entering the town of Townshend. Once again, this is a small town with a historic village green and most of the buildings date from the early 1800s. I was particularly excited to see the old and very beautiful school house still being used as the elementary school. Right next to it is the **Brick Tavern Bed and Breakfast**, should you want to spend a night or two here. It's probably not a good idea to arrive during school dismissal time as I did. With the high school across the common from the elementary school, this idyllic town can turn into Times Square at the ringing of a bell. My car was inadvertently swept by the tide into the high-school back parking lot and I thought I'd never get out.

The **Townshend Common** is at the intersection of State Route 30 and 35. From here, it is about 10 miles north on State Route 35 to the beautifully preserved historic **Grafton**. The road splits about four miles from Townshend and you must bear left at the fork, which will lead you directly into Grafton.

The scenery becomes quite nice as you approach the village and you can't miss the **Grafton Village Cheese Company** on your right. It is a great place to stop, not only to visit the shop and watch the cheese being made, but to walk through the covered bridge and follow the footpath along the stream and meadow – a perfect place to be on an autumn day.

Immediately after the cheese shop, you will see the buildings for the **Windham Foundation**. Here, you can visit the historical exhibits and natural history displays. A stone's throw up the road is the **Gallery North Star**, known for its representation of quality Vermont artists.

The road intersects shortly thereafter with State Route 121, which is also Grafton's Main Street. The only way to truly enjoy such a village as this is on foot. So get out and get a better look at some of the homes, many of which were built in the early 19th century. Thanks to the Windham Foundation, most of them in and around the center have been impeccably preserved and are, without exception, full of classic beauty. There is a general store in the center, a library and a few bed and breakfasts in addition to lodging and dining at The Old Tavern, on the corner of Main Street and State Route 35. If you decide to stay here, you will be added to the long list of travelers that includes Ulysses S. Grant, Ralph Waldo Emerson and Rudyard Kipling.

Take State Route 35 back to Townshend and take a right onto State Route 30. The West River will be on your left and, after a short mile, you will come to the well-known **Scott covered bridge**.

Built in 1870, it is hailed as the "largest single-span covered bridge in Vermont" at 116 feet. It is a fairly amazing piece of architecture and, of course, I had to also measure this one by my walking stride. To my disappointment, I counted 97 steps (not including the ramps), which made me wonder if the 100-step bridge in West Dummerston is actually longer or perhaps doesn't rate as a single-span bridge. It was nearing lunch time, so it is entirely possible that my less than scientifically accurate stride was a bit more enthusiastic thinking of that peanut butter and jelly sandwich in the car.

Next stop, a half-mile up the road, is the enormous **Townshend Dam**, completed in 1961. There is a large parking area and you can read all about the dam at the site. You can also drive over the dam to the opposite side. You will be able to see the sandy beach and picnic area, but unfortunately the access road closes at summer's end.

# Jamaica

After the town of West Townshend, the road will twist and turn toward Jamaica, five miles on. Once you arrive, turn right toward the elementary school, cross a couple of bridges and you will arrive at **Jamaica State Park**. The park sits on the banks of the West River and offers hiking and nature trails, picnicking, fishing, hunting and, in the summer, swimming.

If it's a good scenic view with a little distance you are looking for, head back up State Route 30 about a mile and turn right at Ball Mountain Dam. You can drive all the way to the dam, which towers over the West River.

# Bondville

When you reach Bondville, five miles up from Jamaica on State Route 30, you will also be at the base of **Stratton Mountain**. To go up the mountain, take a left onto Stratton Mountain Road at the large sign.

It is difficult to put into words what happens between Bondville and **Stratton Mountain Resort** near the summit, but you may as well be leaving behind the Vermont we have so far described. In the 15 minutes or so that it takes to climb the mountain by car, you may feel that you have entered into another time and space. Certainly to us rural Vermonters it could easily be another planet. I had never been up the mountain before and had no idea what to expect.

The first thing that one realizes is that Stratton is more than a ski resort. It is a virtual city, offering everything from pro tennis, golf, mountain biking and concerts along with wining and dining. It also offers some spectacular fall foliage viewing from a gondola that rides to the 3,936-foot summit. In addition, there's the annual **Stratton Mountain Arts Festival**, which runs for about a month beginning the last week of September.

From Bondsville to Manchester, State Route 30 is generally downhill and uneventful. You may, however, welcome the calm, for the storm of popular Manchester is less than a half-hour away.

Ignore the signs for Route 7 and continue on State Route 30, which will bring you directly onto Historic Route 7A and Manchester Center.

# Manchester

Manchester Center, unlike Newfane or Grafton, is not where one would go for peace and tranquillity. It is a major Vermont tourist mecca and has all the shopping to prove it. From the Orvis headquarters to London Fog, it's all here for your shopping pleasure. If you would rather look at books than clothes, be sure to visit the **Northshire Bookstore** in the heart of town. There's plenty of history here as well and one shouldn't miss a visit to **Hildene**, the 412-acre former estate of Robert Todd Lincoln, son of Abraham Lincoln, who lived here until his death in 1926.

You can spend an entire day or more just exploring Manchester Center. If you like to be in the heart of things, you may want to spend a night at the **Equinox Hotel**. It is one of Vermont's most historic hotels, built in 1769. It has 163 guest rooms, a AAA-rated four-diamond restaurant and a tavern that also serves complete meals.

If crowds and shops are not your cup of tea, don't write off the area completely. The hills and towns surrounding Manchester are as beautiful as anywhere and there are plenty of quiet out-of-the-way bed and breakfasts to suit any taste.

The well-known and highly respected **Southern Vermont Art Center** is just a 10-minute drive from the center of town, about four miles northwest on State Route 30 and then left onto West Road. The center was once a private estate built in 1917. The estate was put up for sale in 1950 and purchased by the Southern Vermont Artists, Inc. Besides the permanent collection of over 700 works of art (which unfortunately cannot all be displayed at once), the center offers numerous and varied exhibitions, travel and study programs, workshops, special events and concerts.

If you have no interest in the arts, a visit to the center is still highly recommended as the grounds itself are fabulous, including the mile-long twisting driveway which passes through a beautiful section of woods full of birches. If you want to hike, try the 32-year-old **Boswell Botany Trail**, full of trees, ferns and wildflowers, each with an identification marker. Don't forget to look for the 287-year-old sugar maple in the Sculpture Garden. The walk takes a half-hour and an informational brochure is available at the reception desk.

# Dorset

For further exploration, keep traveling northwest on State Route 30 toward Pawlet and the New York border. The Dorset area is nice, but for some truly spectacular scenery keep on going. I found the best views are between East Rupert and North Pawlet as one follows the Mettawee River. You won't see much of the river, however, until after Pawlet (stop in town to admire the art at **Jay Conaway Art Center**). If you're lucky enough to have some good weather and happen to travel this route in late afternoon when the sun is low, you're in for a memorable drive. The setting sun behind those western hills reduces the brilliantly colored trees to a soft and hazy shimmering wall of pastel colors. Unfortunately, there aren't many places to pull the car over, so you may find it difficult to drive and take it all in at the same time. If you have a companion, my advice would be to switch drivers on the way back. It may take some bribing though. Should you want to return to Manchester by a different route, take the right-hand turn onto State Route 133 at Pawlet. After a mile and a half, bear right toward Danby. This road will eventually bring you out to Route 7, at which point you can head south toward Manchester. Watch for **Emerald Lake State Park** on your right. You'll see for yourself how the lake got its name!

If you need gas while in the area, beware. Your credit cards are worthless at a couple of the gas stations and general stores – I found out the hard way.

Leaving Manchester on Route 7A south, you will pass more inns and hotels, both big and small, integrated with historic residential homes. Across the street from the Equinox Hotel is the equally large **Equinox Village Shops**. All this is not to be confused with the **Equinox Mountain Inn**, atop Mt. Equinox farther down the road. If you are interested in driving to the top of **Mt. Equinox**, watch for the signs for the "Skyline Drive" on your right about six miles out of town. This is a toll road and you will have to pay $6 per car to drive up. There is a 360° view from the 3,835-foot summit and, in good weather, you will be able to see into four states.

An alternative route out of Manchester heading south would be to take the Richville Road, turning off State Route 11/30 near Manchester Square. Follow this south to River Road and take a left to Arlington. You will cross the Chiselville Covered Bridge and escape much of the traffic while enjoying some back-road foliage.

# Arlington

Arlington is as beautiful a town as they come and should be explored on foot. It's an experience in itself just to walk down the sidewalks along Main Street, swishing through the fallen maple leaves, taking in the classic beauty of the town Norman Rockwell chose to make his home from 1939 to 1953. It will be hard to miss the **Norman Rockwell Museum** dedicated to this famous artist and illustrator, which stands near the center of town. While there are just a few originals inside, you will be able to view a copy of each *Saturday Evening Post* cover he ever painted. Some of Rockwell's former models now serve as guides to the museum and will be happy to share an anecdote or two with you.

# Shaftsbury

Shaftsbury, former home (one of them, anyway) of poet Robert Frost, has several points of interest to autumn travelers. The **Shaftsbury State Park**, right off Route 7A, offers picnicking and nature trails if you really want to get into the woods. And on East Road, the **Peter Matteson Tavern** hosts the annual Apple and Harvest Festival held in late September. The activities usually include a farmers' market and demonstrations of 18th-century crafts, including cooking and children's activities. For more information, call the Bennington Museum.

# Bennington

From Shaftsbury, you are just a short ride to the rather large city of Bennington. I've gotten myself lost here on more than one occasion, even if I'm just passing through. There is, however, plenty to see and do if you can find your way around town. The Battle of Bennington Monument and the Bennington Museum are popular stops.

On Route 7, 1½ miles south of town, you can visit **The Apple Barn**, a worthwhile stop if you are in the market for some fall goodies, including homemade pies, fresh-picked apples, apple cider and Vermont cheddar cheese.

Our southern Vermont loop takes us out of Bennington via State Route 9, heading back east again toward Brattleboro. As you will discover, State Route 9 is a road that can't make up its mind. It twists to the right, then to the left, uphill, downhill and sideways. The pace at times can be fast. This is a major route – the only direct one – between Bennington and Brattleboro. Despite this, there are numerous opportunities for scenic views, exploration and recreation.

**Woodford State Park** lies about seven miles east of Bennington on Route 9. This is a good stop should you need a little quiet time in the autumn woods. The park offers nature trails, fishing, hunting and camping.

Ten miles beyond the park, the white "Welcome to Wilmington" sign greets you three miles before the center of town. The Deerfield River, which you had only glimpses of before, suddenly opens up into the beautiful and undeveloped **Harriman Reservoir**. There are two places where you can stop to enjoy a good view of this elongated, snake-like body of water, which runs a good six or seven miles in length.

If you want to take a canoe out on the reservoir, look no further than across the street to the **Green Mountain Flagship Company Ltd.** Should a canoe be too small for your taste, then inquire about the large tour boat which cruises the length of the reservoir. There are usually two or three departures daily, with the times posted outside.

# Wilmington

First settled by pioneers in the 1700s, the village of Wilmington is well worth at least a short visit. Again, you should certainly be on foot. The town is full of early American architecture covering the complete range of 19th-century styles. The earliest building in town is the **Norton House** (now a fabric and quilting store) built in 1760.

You may feel as if you've had too much to drink as you walk down South Main Street, but it's probably just the crooked steeple on the former **Unitarian Church**. The church is a shop now and worth a visit for the architecture alone. Just beyond is **Pette Memorial Library**, followed by the town park. If you continue down this road by car, there's a nice little picnic area right on the water.

Cross Route 9 and head up Route 100 north to say hello to Peter at the **Bartleby's Book and Music Store**. I found a better-than-average selection here with some hard-to-find titles readily available. If you continue up this road by car, you can reach Stratton and eventually West Townshend. However, I found the road rather tedious and uninteresting, especially after Dover.

There are several restaurants in Wilmington as well as a handful of inns. For an overnight or a meal, you may want to try the **Old Red Mill Inn** on the river, originally constructed as a saw mill around 1828.

Before you leave the area completely, I should mention the wonderful "Nepco" picnic area about a mile down on Route 100 heading south. It's a large grassy spot right on the reservoir with its own beach, picnic tables and portable facilities.

Heading east again on Route 9, halfway between Wilmington and Marlboro, it will be impossible to miss the **Hogback Mountain** look-out area and the **Skyline Restaurant**. During foliage season in particular, you will most likely run into a minor traffic jam of sorts as cars pull off the road to take in the hundred-mile view. It faces south and east and, on a clear day, one can see the Holyoke Range in Massachusetts as well as New Hampshire's Mt. Monadnock.

Across from the Skyline Restaurant, sitting atop the hill on the north side of the street, is the gift shop and a surprisingly fine **wildlife museum**. The museum is housed in the same building as the gift shop (which explains why I have driven by it year after year and never knew it was there). The small museum is most notable for its excellent collection of stuffed birds, but there are other stuffed animals that are of interest as well. Don't miss the albino deer that was struck by a car in Brattleboro. (One might think a totally white deer would have something going for it when it came to crossing the street, night or day, but maybe this one crossed during a snow storm.) From here, Route 9 will bring you to Interstate 91 or back into Brattleboro.

# For More Information
## *(Area code 802)*

**In Brattleboro**

| | |
|---|---|
| Apple Days Festival | ☎ 254-4565 |
| Brattleboro Chamber of Commerce | ☎ 254-4565 |
| Farmer's Market | ☎ 254-9567 |
| Foliage Crafts Fair | ☎ 254-6734 |
| Music and Art Center | ☎ 257-0124 |
| Windham Brewery | ☎ 254-4747 |

**In Grafton**

| | |
|---|---|
| Gallery North Star | ☎ 843-2465 |
| Grafton Village Cheese Co. Inc. | ☎ 843-2221 |
| Windham Foundation | ☎ 843-2211 |

**In Jamaica**

| | |
|---|---|
| Jamaica State Park, Jamaica | ☎ 874-4600 |

**In Stratton**

| | |
|---|---|
| Stratton Arts Festival | ☎ 297-3265 |
| Stratton Mountain Resort | ☎ 297-4000 |

**In Manchester**

| | |
|---|---|
| Harvest and Craft Festival | ☎ 362-1788 |
| Hildene | ☎ 362-1788 |
| Manchester Chamber of Commerce | ☎ 362-2100 |
| Northshire Bookstore | ☎ 362-2200 |
| Southern Vermont Art Center | ☎ 362-1405 |

**In Arlington**

| | |
|---|---|
| Norman Rockwell Exhibition & Gift Shop | ☎ 375-6423 |

**In Shaftsbury**

| | |
|---|---|
| Shaftsbury State Park | ☎ 375-9978 |

**In Pawlet**

| | |
|---|---|
| Jay Conaway Art Gallery | ☎ 325-3707 |

**In East Dorset**

| | |
|---|---|
| Emerald Lake State Park | ☎ 362-1655 |

**In Bennington**

| | |
|---|---|
| The Apple Barn | ☎ 447-7780 |
| Annual Apple Festival | ☎ 447-1571 |
| Bennington Chamber of Commerce | ☎ 375-9403 |
| Bennington Museum | ☎ 447-1571 |

**In Woodford**

| | |
|---|---|
| Woodford State Park | ☎ 447-7169 |

**In Wilmington**
Bartleby's Book & Music Store ☎ 464-5425
Green Mtn Flagship Co. ☎ 464-2975
Norton House ☎ 464-7213
**In Marlboro**
Skyline Restaurant ☎ 464-3536

## For Accommodations
*(Area code 802)*

**In Brattleboro**
Latchis Hotel ☎ 254-6300
**In Townshend**
Boardman House Bed and Breakfast ☎ 365-4086
**In West Townshend**
Windham Hill Inn ☎ 874-4080
**In Grafton**
The Inn at Woodchuck Hill Farm ☎ 843-2398
The Old Tavern ☎ 843-2231
**In Manchester**
Equinox Hotel ☎ 362-4700
Equinox Mountain Inn ☎ 362-1113
**In Arlington**
Hill Farm Inn ☎ 375-2269
The Evergreen Inn ☎ 375-2272
**In Wilmington**
Le Petit Chef ☎ 464-8437
Nutmeg Inn ☎ 464-3351
Old Red Mill Inn ☎ 464-3700

# Central Vermont Loop

 To get to Montpelier from Interstate 89, take the Montpelier exit into the center of town. Peak foliage is expected during the first week of October.

> **Highlights:** *Covered bridges, Floating Bridge, waterfall, fish hatchery, village greens, Plymouth Notch Historic District, Billing's Farm, Vermont Raptor Center, "World's Fair," Rock of Ages Quarry, chairlift rides and more. (This is the longest outing in the book, covering much of central Vermont.)*

This loop could be explored in a weekend trip or stretched over several days, depending on your interests. The starting point is **Montpelier**, with the excursion heading southward.

## Northfield Falls

Our trip begins by following Route 12 south from the center of Montpelier. Within five minutes, you have left the city behind and are rolling through corn and dairy farms, with the Dog River by your side. About six miles out of Montpelier, a sign will welcome you to Northfield Falls. There are three covered bridges on Cox Brook Road, adjacent to the Falls General Store. The bridges are perfect for photographing because you can look through the first bridge and see the second. This is the only place in New England where two covered bridges can be seen at once. These first two bridges were built around 1872.

# Central Vermont Loop

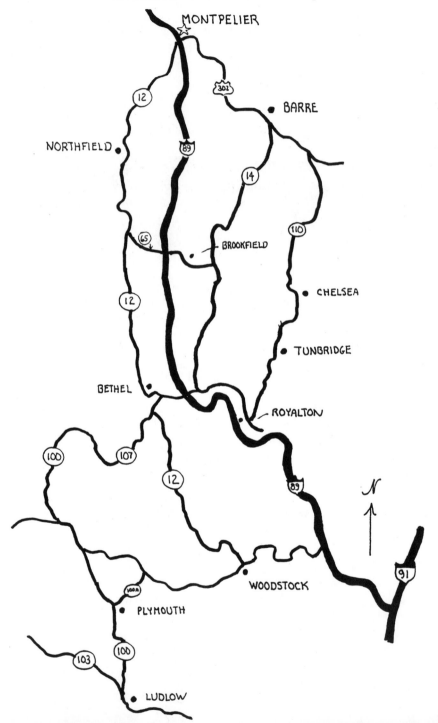

The village green by Northfield University is quite handsome, surrounded by a white rail fence and fine old homes. There are benches on the common and more than once I've stopped here to have a bite to eat while fishing the Dog River. There are a number of dirt roads nearby where it's fun to get lost. Those who ramble these back roads will be rewarded by all sorts of interesting photo opportunities, especially when autumn's colors are splashed on the hardwoods.

# Brookfield

Our next stop is also a bridge, but amazingly this bridge floats! To reach the **floating bridge** at Brookfield, continue on Route 12 exactly 5.3 miles from where it splits with Route 12A. A sign for the bridge will direct you to turn left on a back road. The bridge is at Sunset Lake, 3½ miles farther. The bridge floats on 380 barrels and is 320 feet long. Although you can drive over the bridge, I find that walking is the better way to fully appreciate this structure. Standing mid-point on the bridge is a great way to enjoy a 360° view of fall's color. The last time I walked the bridge, I had the good fortune to meet a gentleman fishing for trout and he told me about more interesting back roads to explore. There was a time when I'd choose fishing over any other pursuit, but these days my passion is discovering new country roads. Like fishing, it's the thrill of seeing and learning new things in an outdoor setting that appeals to me.

At the end of the bridge is the **Green Trails Inn**, a Cape Cod-style farmhouse dating back to 1830 and a large guest house built in 1790. The inn has 14 rooms, decorated in "comfortable elegance," and prides itself on fine cooking. For a relaxing, romantic getaway, this is the place to be. I've stayed here in the spring and had a wonderful time hiking the many trails in the wooded hills behind the inn and resting my weary muscles in my room's private jacuzzi. Nearby roads are excellent to explore by bicycle and friends of mine have enjoyed combining an autumn stay at the inn with a bike trip. In fact, bicycling from inn to inn is quite popular and both Vermont Bicycle Touring and Bike Vermont offer trips all over the state.

From the floating bridge, follow Route 65 east, then turn onto Route 14 south. This is a seldom-used road, but it is quite scenic, passing by cornfields, red barns, dairy cows, white Congregational churches and covered bridges. While it's hard to miss the flaming orange, red and yellow of maples and other hardwoods, keep an eye out for the striking, ocher-yellow tamaracks or larches growing at the edge of a marsh, especially when surrounded by dark spruce. There are few things that visualize the beauty of the north country better than the soft golden color of tamaracks reflected off the smooth surface of water.

# Bethel

When you reach Route 107, follow that southwestward into Bethel. Here, you can visit **Rathdowney Herbs**, which sells everything from herbs to coffees. Also in Bethel is the **White River National Fish Hatchery**, with a visitors room inside and large holding pools filled with trout and salmon outside.

# Pittsfield

Soon, Route 107 intersects with Route 100, which you should follow to the south, traveling through Pittsfield with its rectangular green surrounded by homes painted white, as so many of the older homes are in New England. You will also pass the **Giorgetti Covered Bridge**, lovingly built by John Giorgetti in 1976 using material from an old barn. Much of the land around Route 100 is forested and there is good hiking at **Gifford Woods State Park**, just before the intersection with Route 4. **Killington** and **Pico ski areas** are also near this intersection. Killington operates a chairlift during foliage season for spectacular views and Pico has an alpine slide and scenic chairlift.

# Plymouth Union, Ludlow & Bridgewater

Continuing south on Route 100 you will reach the village of Plymouth Union (a village within the town of Plymouth), where you should turn left on Route 100A to reach **Plymouth Notch Historic District**, a beautiful place in an idyllic setting, nestled high in a mountain notch. This rural Vermont village was the birthplace of Calvin Coolidge, the 30th president of the United States. The entire village is included on the National Register of Historic Places and remains virtually unchanged since the turn of the century.

Here, you can visit the **Coolidge Birthplace**, attached to the general store. President Coolidge was born in the downstairs bedroom on July 4, 1872. Nearby is the **Coolidge Homestead**, into which the family moved when Calvin was four years old. Later, during Coolidge's term as vice-president, he was vacationing here when word came of the unexpected death of President Warren Harding. Coolidge's father was a notary public and it was he who administered the presidential oath of office to his son at 2:47 a.m. on August 3, 1923. Today, the rooms are furnished exactly as they were at that time.

There are dozens of other interesting buildings and exhibits in the village. The 1830 **Wilder House**, formerly a tavern, now serves as a small restaurant and across the street is the **Wilder Barn**, which has exhibits of 19th-century farm implements. Cheese is still made at the **Plymouth Cheese Factory**, built by the president's father in 1890. A one-room schoolhouse stands next to the factory and it too dates back to 1890. The entire village is so inviting and tastefully maintained that it's a wonder we have not preserved more culturally significant towns.

By continuing your exploration south down Route 100, you will reach its intersection with Route 103. One of nature's grand sights awaits nearby. Turn right onto Route 103 and then take the first right onto Buttermilk Falls Road. You guessed it –

**Buttermilk Falls** is straight ahead. If you love waterfalls as much as I do, you won't want to miss this one. Water cascades over a wide granite ledge and enters a crystal-clear pool framed by hemlock and maples. When the sun hits the falls and lights up the trees, have your camera ready.

Our ramble continues by retracing our trail north to the intersection with Route 4, where you should head east. Be sure to check out the various country stores along the way, especially if you are looking for unique gifts. There are all sorts of fine inns and motels in the area, but during foliage season they are booked solid, so be sure to make reservations. I brought my family to the **October Country Inn** one season and we had a wonderful stay. The food was excellent, the atmosphere casual and the grounds beautiful, with apple trees, an old-fashioned swing and a pool situated high up on a hillside. The innkeepers seemed to think of all the little things, like placing night lights in our rooms for the kids.

# Woodstock

Where Routes 4, 12 and 106 converge is the village of Woodstock, which is famous for its charm, boutiques, restaurants and picture-perfect scenery. But be warned that it also attracts crowds during autumn. History buffs may want to visit the Woodstock Historical Society's **Dana House Museum**, which focuses on the culture of central Vermont. Inside the Federal-style house on Elm Street, look at the decorative arts, furniture, paintings, historic costumes, toys and textiles. There is also a gift shop with uncommon gifts inspired by artifacts from the museum.

Just outside the center of Woodstock, off Route 12 North, is the **Billings Farm & Museum**, a working farm with two floors of exhibits. Children will enjoy the various farm animals and a twice-daily milking of the cows. Inside the 1890 farmhouse, you can learn how it functioned as the hub of farm operations a century ago.

*Above:* Down the Road.

*Below:* Fairfield Road.

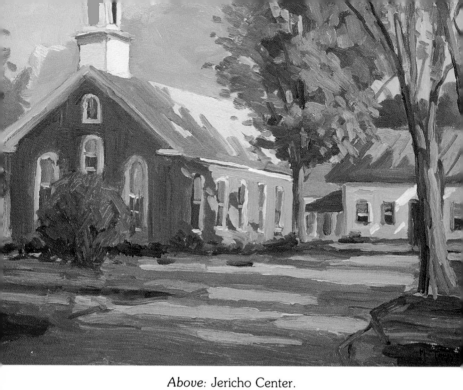

*Above:* Jericho Center.

*Below:* Mount Mansfield View.

*Above:* Autumn Reflections.

*Below:* After the Rain.

*Above:* Autumn Hills.

*Below:* Bakersfield View.

The **Vermont Raptor Center** is also near town on Church Hill Road. This living museum introduces visitors to the hawks and owls of northern New England. The birds here have permanent injuries that prevent their being released into the wild. There are over 40 live birds, including a bald eagle, peregrine falcon and a tiny saw-whet owl.

From Woodstock, we continue north, this time on Route 12. The road is filled with great views, first following Gulf Stream and later **Locust Brook**, where you may want to try your luck angling for trout. Brook trout are especially active in the fall when they breed and their colors brighten like the leaves, turning orange on their belly, with deep red spots on their flanks. The practice of catch-and-release lets you enjoy the sport, while keeping it productive for future anglers. Locust Brook is a classic mountain stream and affords some great photo opportunities.

Where Route 12 intersects Route 107, turn right passing back into Bethel and then south on Route 14. In the small center of Royalton is a sign describing **The Royalton Raid**: "October 16, 1780. To terrorize the valley from Tunbridge to Royalton, nearly three hundred Indians led by a British officer fell on these defenseless settlements, killing four, taking twenty-six prisoners and reducing Royalton to ashes. Captives were hauled back to Canada and were sold for $8 a head." Historic signs like this add so much to a town center, as do the old buildings. Royalton has a tiny red brick library and two old churches. The town common, however, is located in South Royalton and that's where we go next.

# South Royalton

Route 14 parallels the White River and there is a wide shoulder on the right side of the road overlooking a small waterfall. This is a good place to stop the car if you want to get a better look at the river. At the intersection with Route 110, turn right and cross the river into South Royalton. The large square common has a gazebo and benches and is encircled by old homes and shops. An old maple tree at the west end of the common always seems to show its color first and, during my last visit in early September, it was already streaked with orange. There is a pizza shop and restaurant (a good place to stop for lunch), as well as the **South Royalton House**, owned and operated by the Vermont Law School, which serves sandwiches and salads. Housed in a handsome gray wooden building with red shutters, the South Royalton House, built in 1850, helps give the center of town a stately look.

# Tunbridge

Covered bridges begin to appear with regularity as you leave South Royalton and follow Route 110 north into Tunbridge. The first covered bridge you pass is the **Howe Bridge**, erected in 1879. I've read that bridges were covered to keep snow and ice off the wooden planks so horses wouldn't slip. Another theory said that horses feared crossing water at a height and by covering a bridge the horse would get the impression of entering a barn. But the real reason was good old Yankee practicality: covering the bridge protects the structural members in the span. Periodic replacement of the roof is far simpler (and cheaper) than repairing the timbers below.

When passing through Tunbridge, you can't help but notice the sign for the "**World's Fair**," held annually since 1867 in mid-September. It's an old-fashioned agricultural fair featuring such events as pony- and ox-pulling, livestock displays, collections of old-time relics, dancing, sulky racing and fiddler contests. Organizing a trip to coincide with the fair might be the perfect way to see rural Vermont and early fall color. (It's called the World's Fair as the events are open to contestants worldwide.)

Just beyond the Tunbridge town hall is the **Mill Covered Bridge** (1883) with a sign over the entrance reading "One dollar fine for a person to drive a horse or other beast faster than a walk or drive

more than one loaded team at the same time on this bridge."
Two more covered bridges, the Larkin Bridge and Moxley Bridge,
are alongside Route 110 a bit farther to the north. A nice
combination of pasture, forest and rivers makes this section
especially scenic.

# Chelsea

The **Shire Inn**, a beautiful Federal-style home built in 1832,
is located in Chelsea and looks like a great spot to use as a base
for those interested in exploring this part of Vermont. From the
inn you can walk to Chelsea center, a quintessential New England
town, with two village greens situated side by side. Big maples
grow here, making the greens especially colorful in the fall. The
simplicity of this village and the feeling that it's been untouched
by time make it a special place.

# Barre

More scenic views await as you head northward on Route 110
into Barre. At the junction of Route 110 and 302, follow the
signs to the **Rock of Ages Quarry**. This is the world's largest
granite quarry, dating back over one hundred years. A 30-minute
shuttle tour takes you through the quarries, while the
manufacturing operations can be seen from an observation deck.
Some of the stone cut from the quarry can be seen at the **Hope
Cemetery**, located just 1½ miles up Route 14 from the center
of Barre. There are a number of unique headstones with elaborate
carvings crafted by Vermont's turn-of-the-century stonecutters.

By following Route 302 west, you will have completed the loop
back to Montpelier.

# For More Information
## (Area code is 802 unless noted otherwise)

| | |
|---|---|
| Bike Vermont | ☎ 800-257-2226 |
| Billings Farm and Museum | ☎ 457-2355 |
| Coolidge Birthplace | ☎ 672-3273 |
| Dana House Museum | ☎ 457-1822 |
| Gifford Woods State Park | ☎ 888-5733 |
| Killington (foliage chairlift) | ☎ 773-1330 |
| Pico Alpine Slide | ☎ 775-4346 |
| Plymouth Cheese Factory | ☎ 672-3650 |
| Plymouth Notch Historic District | ☎ 672-3773 |
| Rathdowney Herbs | ☎ 234-9928 |
| Rock of Ages Quarry | ☎ 476-3119 |
| Vermont Bicycle Touring | ☎ 453-4811 |
| Vermont Raptor Center | ☎ 457-2779 |
| White River National Fish Hatchery | ☎ 234-5241 |
| Wilder House | see Coolidge Birthplace |

# For Accommodations
## (Area code is 802 unless noted otherwise)

**In Barre and Montpelier**

Central Vermont Chamber of Commerce ☎ 800-229-4619

**In Bridgewater Corners**

October Country Inn ☎ 672-3412

**In Brookfield**

Birch Meadow Cabins Bed and Breakfast ☎ 276-3156
Green Trails Inn ☎ 276-3412 or 800-243-3412

**In Chelsea**

Shire Inn ☎ 685-3031

**In Killington and Pico**

Killington and Pico Area Association ☎ 773-4181

**In Ludlow**

Governors Inn ☎ 228-8830

**In Northfield**

Four Bridges Inn ☎ 485-8995
Northfield Inn ☎ 485-8558

**In Plymouth**
Farmbrook Motel ☎ 672-3621
Hawk Inn Resort ☎ 800-685-HAWK
Salt Ash Inn ☎ 672-3748
**In Royalton**
Fox Stand Inn ☎ 763-8437
**In Sharon**
The Columns Motor Lodge ☎ 763-7040
**In Woodstock**
Woodstock Chamber of Commerce ☎ 457-3555
The Woodstock Inn & Resort ☎ 457-1100

# Mount Mansfield Loop, Northern Vermont

 From Interstate 89, take exit 10, then head north up State Route 100 for 10 miles to Stowe. This tour begins and ends in Stowe and can be done in one or two days. Peak foliage is expected from October 5th to 11th.

**Highlights:** *Stowe, Vermont's tallest mountain, gondola ride, Smuggler's Notch, Jeffersonville, Waterville, foliage train ride, Pleasant Valley, St. Albans, maple-sugar country, dairy farms, covered bridges, Cold Hollow Cider Mill, Ben and Jerry's ice cream factory, Old Red Mill, art galleries, rolling hills and open fields.*

## Stowe

If you are an avid skier, then you most likely have heard about Stowe, if not having already been to this eastern United States ski capital. This tour begins in Stowe a month before the first snow, but don't be surprised should you see the gleaming white powder atop towering Mount Mansfield as early as mid-October. As far as weather is concerned, it's a different ball game up there. Similar to Manchester in its ability to attract tourists, Stowe is a unique world unto itself. The people of Stowe have worked hard, and succeeded, at keeping the immediate downtown area a real working, living Vermont village in spite of the 300,000 tourists who come annually. Traffic will surely move slowly during the tourist seasons, but the authentic character and essence of Main Street has been retained. There are plenty of amenities in the area and, if you like the diversity Stowe has to offer, especially with lodging and dining, then you may want to make this your home base for any exploration of the outlying countryside.

## Mount Mansfield Loop

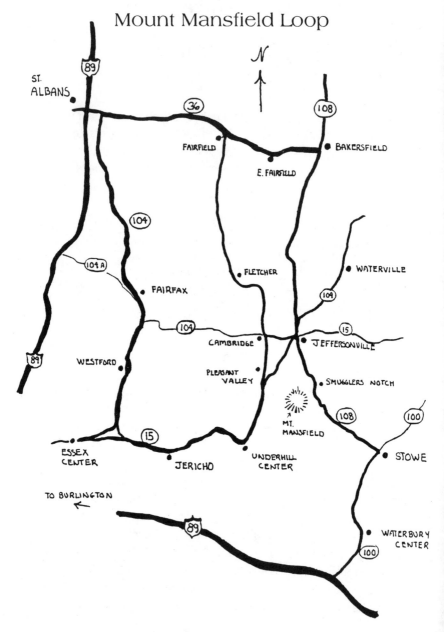

No matter what time of year you visit Stowe, there seems always to be some kind of fair or event. During the last days of August, the Helen Day Art Center sponsors the enormously popular "**A Taste of Stowe**," a wonderful blend of the area's artists and restaurants all under one roof. In late September, you may catch the annual **Stowe Foliage Craft Fair**, featuring crafts, great food, musicians and comedy. Call the Stowe Area Association before leaving home. When in town, pick up a copy of "The Stowe Guide," available at most shops.

Just outside of town on State Route 100 heading south, you can visit Vermont's largest producer of fresh apple cider: the **Cold Hollow Cider Mill**. It's an interesting place to stop, featuring the cider-making process and a gift shop full of Vermont specialty foods.

If ice cream is your weakness, then you won't want to miss **Ben and Jerry's ice cream factory** and headquarters in **Waterbury**, just down the road, also on State Route 100. You can learn about the history of Ben and Jerry's famous specialty, browse through the gift shop, take a tour, watch the process of making ice cream and, of course, stock up on goodies.

Also running the length of State Route 100, right into downtown Stowe, there are numerous antique shops. If you are arriving from Interstate 89, you may want to take some of these in before you reach Stowe (our actual Mount Mansfield loop trip heads in the opposite direction).

Before leaving Stowe altogether, make sure you spend some time on the **Stowe Recreation Path**. The 5½-mile paved trail for walking or biking is a great way to enjoy the immediate countryside outside of your car. The entrance parking is just off Main Street behind the Community Church.

Book lovers will enjoy **Bear Pond Books** on Main Street and, for the serious art connoisseur or collector, a visit to **Clarke Galleries** is a must. The gallery features 19th- and early 20th-century paintings. It's on the left at the beginning of Mountain Road.

Traveling up Mountain Road (State Route 108) and passing an endless array of resorts, you will find the entrance to the mountain toll road that goes almost to the summit of **Mount Mansfield**. Or, if you want to save your car from exhaustion and you are not afraid of heights, take the new eight-passenger gondola (claimed to be the world's fastest) found at the Mansfield Base Lodge. A reminder that at 4,393 feet, Mount Mansfield is Vermont's highest peak (followed by Killington Peak at 4,241 feet).

Driving on State Route 108 over **Smuggler's Notch** is an experience in itself. It won't be difficult to see why this mountain pass is closed during the winter months. Even in good weather, you will have no choice other than to drive extremely slow as you near the peak and enter another world and ecosystem. If you sneeze or blink, you may find yourself in serious trouble on these hairpin turns where there is no margin for error. You may notice a sudden change in temperature, as well as find yourself among the clouds. If there is a cloud in the sky, chances are it will be here, clinging to the peak. Fortunately, there are a few places to pull the car over, get out and hike around to enjoy this unusual spot. You may even spot a peregrine falcon, reportedly they nest in the area.

# Jeffersonville

Once over the notch, as you head downhill, you will pass the alpine slide at Spruce Peak followed by Smuggler's Notch Resort. This is the last of the big resorts you will see for awhile as you descend into Jeffersonville. You are now somewhere over the rainbow and a long way from the bustle of Stowe.

Near the very end of your steep descent, a stone's throw from the village proper, you can visit the **Brewster River Gristmill** on your right. This is a working mill, as well as a small gift shop for Vermont products. The beautiful old covered bridge which you will see spanning the Brewster River has long been a favorite among local artists. From here, you can walk along the river and try your luck at catching some of the big trout that like to congregate in the pools. I've seen them many times while swimming here with my goggles, unsuccessfully trying to catch them by hand.

Jeffersonville, which is on the National Register of Historic Preservation, is an interesting and pleasant little town. It has long been a gathering place for landscape painters from both near and far, especially those from Massachusetts and the Cape Ann area. For over 60 years, painters have come to capture the diverse views of hills, rivers, fields, bridges and towns which make this area so special. They are still coming today and, after you do a little exploring, you will see why.

There are two art galleries in town, diagonally across from one another on Main Street. One is the **Mary Bryan Memorial Art Gallery** and the other is the **Silver Wing Art Gallery**. Both feature various exhibitions of regional artists.

Also on Main Street near the galleries, you can't miss the Windridge Bakery and the five-star restaurant, Le Cheval d'Ors. And for quilts, go no farther than **Quilts by Elaine**, right next to Silver Wing Art Gallery.

The **Second Congregational Church**, on the corner of Main and Church Streets, is a replica of one that burned to the ground in 1993.

If you prefer to stay overnight on this side of the mountain, then the **Smuggler's Notch Inn** might be just the place for you. Across from the church, the 200-year-old inn is intimate and full of character. It is also a good place to stop for lunch or dinner. A less formal place to get a good bite to eat is Jana's Cupboard on State Route 15 just down the road from the inn.

# Waterville

One of my favorite stretches of road in this area is on State Route 15 from Jeffersonville to Johnson. Unfortunately, the pace can be fast here and there are few places to pull over. Nevertheless, the views of the valley to your left with the mountain backdrop are really wonderful, especially if you like open spaces. The river you will see here is the Lamoille. Go as far as you like and return via the Hogback Road, which will take you along the ridge on the opposite side of the river. This road will bring you directly onto State Route 109 and into the beautiful town of Waterville. With maple trees being plentiful, this entire area is truly spectacular in autumn. I've met people from all over the country here; they come for good reason.

If covered bridges interest you, then you have come to the right place. There are five of them within the eight miles between here and Belvedere on State Route 109. And if you still can't get enough, there are plenty more if you head up toward Montgomery.

After having explored the Waterville area, head south on State Route 109, which will bring you to State Route 108. From here there are two ways to go. If you prefer paved roads and a more direct route, without the possibility of becoming lost, then travel north on State Route 108 into Bakersfield. In Bakersfield, take a left onto State Route 36 heading west toward Fairfield and eventually St. Albans. If you are a bit more daring and don't mind dirt roads and making a few wrong turns, then take a left and get back onto State Route 15. Before you enter Cambridge, you will arrive at what's locally known as the "**wrong way bridge**," a relatively dangerous intersection (you will probably recognize it when you are there). Don't go over the bridge. Instead, bear right and keep going straight toward Fletcher. You may make a few wrong turns as the road tends to curve this way and that, but if you make it to the Fletcher Grange, about eight miles up on your left, then you are on the right track. Four miles or so after that, the road will cut sharply to the left and go downhill. Follow this road another 10 miles into Fairfield. If you are able to do this successfully, then you will have passed "driving in rural Vermont 101" with flying colors. You will have passed through the heart of dairy country and maple-sugar land. There are numerous old and very beautiful farms, barns and sugar shacks dotting the open hillsides. Don't forget to look behind you for some awesome views of Mount Mansfield. You won't be disappointed.

# Fairfield

At Fairfield Center, the road you are on intersects with State Route 36. On your right, there is an old brick building recently renovated into a country store and, on your left, the **Fairfield Center School**. To head toward St. Albans, take a left here and enjoy the open countryside used for grazing cows, of which there are plenty.

The nature of the autumn sky is to be full of charcoal clouds that cast enormous shadows upon hill and field. The sun, so much like a heavenly spotlight, casts its singular rays upon a distant hillside, setting it ablaze with fiery light. I once witnessed a narrow beam of light, like a solid form, break through a completely overcast deep gray-blue sky and stay on the peaked summit of a large distant mountain. This, I thought to myself, could happen only in autumn. What a glorious and never-ending show of sunlight and shadow all around us. Showtime is everyday of the year and the admission is free.

The road to St. Albans gradually rises and falls and will become flat just as you pass the Fairfield Marsh, which fans out on both sides. After this, the road resumes its rolling again until you reach the ultimate downhill experience, the **Fairfield Hill**. Save your brakes by putting your car into low gear and enjoy the spectacular view. This hill offers a grand glimpse into the Champlain Valley and beyond. Not only will you view Lake Champlain and the islands, but you'll also see well into New York State and the Adirondacks.

# St. Albans

Known as the capital of the maple-sugaring industry, St. Albans is a good stop-over on our visit through this corner of Vermont. Among the row of historic brick buildings that run along the common is the **Historical Museum**. The building was formerly a grade school built in 1861. Take a peek inside and find out about the famous confederate raid on the town in 1864 or see Dr. Beaumont's office as it was depicted in the famous Norman Rockwell painting. There's plenty more, including artifacts from various periods in the local history.

Spend some time visiting the shops on Main Street and stop in at Jeff's Maine Seafood for a great lunch or order something to go and drive up Congress Street to reach the **Hard'ack Recreational Area**, which has hiking trails and a good view from Aldis Hill.

To see the real flat lands, head down Lake Street toward **St. Albans Bay**. You will reach the lake named after Samuel de Champlain who explored the area in 1609. Drive beyond St. Albans Bay State Park and bear left on Hathaway Point Road to reach the much nicer **Kill Kare State Park**, a former boys' camp on this windy peninsula.

From St. Albans, it's 62 miles to Montreal, but this tour now heads south. Leave St. Albans the way you came in. State Route 104 intersects State Route 36 at the foot of the Fairfield Hill. Make a right turn onto State Route 104 south.

Only a minute's drive out of town, the wide-open landscape begs attention. The Fairfield ridge will be on your left, while down to your right deep green and ochre pastures lure you onward.

Eventually, you will pass the junction of State Route 104A on your right, which takes you to the interstate, but don't be tempted. Nothing on the highway can compare with the views and rural scenery along the road you're already on. Shortly after passing State Route 104A, the Buck Hollow Road begins on your left. This is as scenic a road as any and will take you to **The Inn at Buck Hollow Farm**, a small and intimate family-run inn. The renovated 1790s house is the ideal place to stay if you want to truly escape into these hills.

Back in Fairfax, bear right after passing Berardinelli's General Store, staying on State Route 104 as you cross over Browns River, which provides you with a couple of good river views. Less than a mile on, the road will split again, both routes going to State Route 128. I recommend you go straight. From here, the scenery only gets better and you will be immediately rewarded with a panoramic veiw looking east towards Mount Mansfield. The road then heads downhill for a spell with yet more fabulous views to your left.

Just before reaching the town of Westford, stop at **Applebrook Farms** on your left and say hello to Paul and Caren Birnholz who own and work the farm. In the fall, their open barn is stocked with pumpkins, gourds, Indian corn, preserves, dried flowers and maple syrup. If you are lucky, you may see them making apple cider on their old cider press. If nothing else, the view from their driveway is worth admiring.

# Westford

Westford center must not have changed all that much in the past one hundred years. Even with a new house or two, there remains a distinct 19th-century air to it. Perhaps it is something to do with the silence. It isn't too hard to imagine horse-drawn carriages rattling their way down the dirt road along the village common. To stay on State Route 128, just go around the common to your left and on towards Essex.

You can drive into busy **Essex** by continuing straight until you reach the traffic light, then taking a left onto State Route 15. Or, you can do yourself a favor by taking the unmarked dirt road to your left, at the elbow of a sharp curve on State Route 128. This scenic road will take you directly to State Route 15. Turn left when you reach it. More wonderful autumn countryside awaits you as you approach Jericho.

# Jericho

The **Old Red Mill**, a National Historic Site, lies three miles up the road on your left. This is an excellent place to stop for several reasons. The mill, which dates back to the mid-1800s, contains a craft shop, gallery and museum. Be sure you ask at the front desk for the key to visit the basement, which houses all the old milling machinery and the many products of Jericho's water-powered mills. But it is the outside of the mill that really offers excitement. Here, the **Browns River** thunders and foams through the gorge. It's best seen from the bridge on the road. Next to the parking lot is the entrance to a footpath which follows the river. About four separate pools have formed, each with their own small waterfall – good for fishing, swimming or just relaxing on the boulders. There are picnic tables and a couple of benches facing the river.

Traveling farther on State Route 15, just past the Jericho Elementary School, you will see the giant Mount Mansfield appear in front of you. Depending on the time of day, year and weather, mountains, especially large ones, can be almost any color or combination of colors. It's no wonder artists have been drawn to them over the years.

# Underhill

Traveling east on Route 15, you will eventually come to a sharp left bend. For a more scenic drive with less traffic, I suggest you keep going straight towards Underhill Center, two miles down the road. The Underhill General Store will be on your left, the Town Hall and Historical Society on your right. Camping picnicking, hunting, fishing and some good foot trails can be found at **Underhill State Park**, three miles up the dirt road near the town center. During the last week of September, Underhill holds it annual **Old Fashioned Harvest Market**, complete with a parade, crafts, bands and a country store on the grounds of the United Church in Underhill Flats.

Leaving Underhill, the road is soon swallowed up by a heavily wooded section of predominantly maple and birch trees. This provides a dramatic contrast to the sudden open vistas ahead as you roll downhill into appropriately named **Pleasant Valley**. It's the lay of the land here, pure and simple, which captivates the traveler and nature's ever-changing light is enough to stir the artist in all of us. The views, full of hills and dotted by the occasional farm, are never boring.

The road splits into the Upper Valley Road on your right and the Lower Valley Road to your left. Both are of equal beauty, but it will be worth your while to take the Lower Valley Road so you can visit the town of Cambridge. Don't forget to look behind you to catch some of the most splendid views anywhere of Mount Mansfield. If you can't get enough, return from Cambridge on this road and then take the Upper Valley Road for some more great scenery. This will lead you right into Jeffersonville and to the Smuggler's Notch Inn.

# Cambridge

You will arrive in Cambridge by way of the back door, meeting State Route 15 directly in front of you. It's easy to park the car somewhere near the Cambridge General Store, where you can buy a soda and then walk the length of the long, narrow town common.

When you are ready to leave, head east on State Route 15, go round the bend, pass the old Cambridge covered bridge, cross the river on the "wrong way bridge," and head east again toward Jeffersonville. Stop at the **Vermont Maple Outfit** just ahead on your left for any of your maple-sugar needs. A stone's throw up the road, you can pick up State Route 108 and go right into Jeffersonville and back over the notch into Stowe.

# Morrisville

One final item worthy of mention, but not on our route, is the **Lamoille Valley Railroad** in Morrisville, about a half-hour drive east on State Route 15. The railroad offers a 2½-hour fall foliage trip along the Lamoille River and through one of the few covered railroad bridges still in use. The train runs until October 15th. Call the number on the following page for more information.

## For More Information
*(Area code 802 unless noted otherwise)*

| | |
|---|---|
| Applebrook Farms | ☎ 878-8856 |
| Bear Pond Books | ☎ 253-8236 |
| Ben and Jerry's Ice Cream Factory | ☎ 244-5641 |
| Clarke Galleries, Inc. | ☎ 253-7116 |
| Cold Hollow Cider Mill | ☎ 244-8771 |

| | |
|---|---|
| Jeff's Maine Seafood | ☎ 524-6135 |
| Kill Kare State Park | ☎ 534-6021 |
| Lamoille Valley Railroad | ☎ 888-4255 |
| Mary Bryan Memorial Art Gallery | ☎ 644-5100 |
| The Old Red Mill | ☎ 899-3225 |
| Pleasant Valley Wildlife Sanctuary | ☎ 637-0320 |
| Quilts by Elaine | ☎ 644-5438 |
| St. Albans Chamber of Commerce | ☎ 524-2444 |
| St. Albans Historical Museum | ☎ 527-7933 |
| Silver Wing Art Gallery | ☎ 644-8103 |
| Stowe Area Association | ☎ 800-24STOWE |
| Stowe Foliage Craft Fair | ☎ 253-7321 |
| Underhill State Park | ☎ 899-3022 |
| Underhill Old Fashioned Harvest Market | ☎ 899-3369 |
| Vermont Maple Outfit | ☎ 644-5482 |

# For Accommodations
*(Area code 802 unless noted otherwise)*

**In Stowe**

| | |
|---|---|
| Stowe Inn and Tavern at Little River | ☎ 800-227-1108 |
| Trapp Family Lodge | ☎ 253-8511 |
| Stowe Mtn Resort (gondola, alpine slide) | ☎ 244-5641 |

**In Smuggler's Notch**

| | |
|---|---|
| Smuggler's Notch Resort | ☎ 800-451-8752 |

**In Jeffersonville**

| | |
|---|---|
| Smuggler's Notch Inn | ☎ 644-2412 |

**In Fairfax**

| | |
|---|---|
| The Inn at Buck Hollow Farm | ☎ 849-2400 |

# Northeast Kingdom

 To reach this area from Interstate 91, take exit 21 onto Route 2 west. At Danville, bear right onto State Route 15 heading northwest into Hardwick. The trip begins and ends here and can be done in one day. The peak foliage is expected to be during the first week in October.

**Highlights:** *Barr Hill Nature Preserve, trails, 50-mile views, Lake Willoughby, Crystal Lake, Bread and Puppet Museum, serene old town commons, Old Stone House Museum.*

Like many areas of Vermont, the Northeast Kingdom has its own distinct flavor. Rich in evergreens, it is not the most colorful area of Vermont as far as fall foliage is concerned. You will not see the wall-to-wall blazing oranges, yellows and reds that can so easily be found elsewhere in the state. However, the deep greens of the conifers, mixed with the less frequent maples and birches, provide us with a landscape that has a lot of punch. In fact, a single maple in peak foliage becomes an event among a sea of green. Perhaps fall colors are best appreciated in precisely this setting.

The terrain here is also worthy of note and, to the more perceptive, unique to this area. Among the dense evergreen forests are wide expanses of open, gentle hills and plateaus, such as the ones near Barr Hill in Greensboro, in the Craftsbury Common area and in towns like Irasburg. One can imagine that a century ago there was even more open space here used for pastures and that many of the forested areas we see today are, in fact, quite young. The abundance of some very beautiful lakes and ponds, particularly between State Route 14 to the west and State Route 114 to the east, add greatly to the diversification and enjoyment of this area. Some refer to this area as simply "The

Kingdom" because the land east of I-91 and, in particular east of Route 114, is quite different. This true eastern corner of Vermont has far more forests and is more mountainous, with fewer towns and roads. It is truly a remote and wild area. For a relatively short autumn drive, I've chosen a route more plentiful in open views, rivers, ponds lakes and meadows. The old towns along the way are picturesque, historic and peaceful.

# The Northeast Kingdom

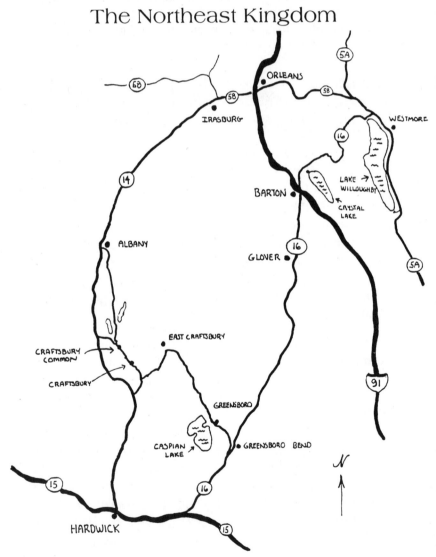

# Hardwick

We begin in Hardwick where the Village Restaurant boasts "home-style cooking." You can't miss it in the center of town at the intersection of State Routes 14 and 15. From here, follow State Route 15 east along the Lamoille River for two miles and then make a left turn onto State Route 16 heading north. About a mile up on your left, follow the first signs to Caspian Lake. This road leads to **Greensboro**.

On your left, directly across from the Historical Society, follow the signs to the public beach. Here, you will enjoy a wide-open view of **Caspian Lake**. It is a nice place to swim in the summer, albeit a cold one. I have painted right on the water's edge, looking out along the shore.

Leaving the beach, take a left past the general store and the town library, bear right at the fork and then left at the next fork, which goes up Barr Hill Road. Continue uphill on this scenic road until you come to the spot where you think you are driving into someone's house. Don't turn around; just keep on going over the little hill and you will see the sign for the **Barr Hill Nature Preserve**. Drive along this sometimes rough dirt road over the beautiful terrain with evergreen trees and maples, meadows and boulders until you reach the parking lot. This is a fabulous spot and you won't regret coming here. You are on top of 2,120-foot Barr Hill, a most inspiring and uplifting place to be on a crisp autumn day.

The trails start here at the parking lot and, if you are lucky, there will be some trail guide maps in the little wooden boxes. Even if you do not intend to hike the trails, at least walk the 30 seconds or so up to point "B," which is marked on the wooden posts. Your reward will be a tremendous view looking south and southwest. An easy-to-read map explains what you are looking at. Mount Mansfield, Camel's Hump, Bread Loaf Mountain, Killington and more are all visible on a clear day. Walk up to point "C" for a nice view of Caspian Lake below. Farther along at point

"L" (if you are not hiking the trail, you can take a short cut by going to the right of the campfire area) is yet another view, this time looking northeast. The panoramic scene is from Bald Mountain to Burke Mountain and, although it may be difficult to spot, take a good look and try to make out the faint ghost of New Hampshire's Mount Washington some 54 miles away.

The scenery and views are just as wonderful as you leave the nature preserve. Driving down the winding road on my way out, I was reminded of a George Innes painting which hangs in the Worcester Art Museum in Massachusetts – with the view as well as the light reminiscent of the little painting. Now there was a great painter, I thought to myself!

# East Craftsbury

Back-track down the Barr Hill Road and take a sharp right up the Craftsbury Road, which begins at the Caspian Lake Grange. This will bring you into East Craftsbury, where there are a couple of bed and breakfasts if you feel like spending a night in this quiet little town. Some of the side roads here are well worth exploring.

As you leave town and go up the hill and around the bend, there is a terrific view looking back down on the village. There are private homes here, so it is not a good place to stop and set up an easel. Such is the case with countless good sites. In fact, just over the past few years alone, I have lost scores of scenic painting spots to development and private homes – maybe good for the economy, but not for the artist.

Go slow as you continue on the main road away from East Craftsbury, not only to enjoy the scenery, but because the road plunges downhill quite suddenly toward a stop sign. Take a right at the sign and, in no time, you will enter the town of **Craftsbury**. This entire area is fun territory to explore and you really can't go wrong. I especially like the bright yellow tamarack trees with their slender curving arms and pointed tops, common in the Northeast Kingdom.

A mile or so down the road, you will arrive at beautiful **Craftsbury Common**, full of spacious, colonial elegance. Park along the town common and enjoy this gem of a town, where every building is painted white. If it is dinner time, you may want to try the **Inn on the Common**, noted for its fine meals and lodging.

Just outside of town is the **Craftsbury Center**, an outdoor sports center offering cross-country skiing, canoeing, rowing, hiking, orienteering for hiking and more.

If Craftsbury Common reminds you too much of a postcard, have no fear – there is always good ol' Albany just up the road on State Route 14. To get there, descend the scenic road on the far side of the common.

# Irasburg

Passing Albany, continue on State Route 14 for 10 minutes to Irasburg. The steeple of the Unification Church can been seen peeking out from among the tree tops as you approach town. Neither like Albany nor Craftsbury Common, Irasburg has a distinction of its own, one of understated grace and simplicity. The way the large town common separates the buildings and homes – and the fact that the town is situated on a plateau of sorts – gives Irasburg an open and spacious feel. I liked the unpretentiousness and the wonderful accessibility of the common.

I remembered that Irasburg was the birthplace of American Impressionist Theodore Robinson. Born here in 1852, he stayed only until he was three years old, hardly enough time to create a masterpiece, but an interesting enough fact for a fellow painter and admirer. I inquired around town about him. Perhaps his home was still standing or someone would know the location where it once stood, or there may even have been relatives, which would not be unusual in a Vermont village. And so to this end I spent the next hour wandering from the closed library to the closed Town Hall to the closed Post Office then back to the library (which had finally opened but, alas, the regular librarian was not in), next over to the general store, where I was told to ask for so-and-so. Unfortunately, no one had ever heard of Robinson, but there was a small paragraph written about him in the town's history book, which proved that my memory wasn't so bad after all. Finally, I was told that there were some old paintings in the Town Hall and, by now, it was an offer I could not refuse. Besides, I would get to see the inside of the old building. And so to the Town Hall I went with Junior (Junior's father happened to be working on the roof and who happened to have the key, which he threw down to us).

The paintings turned out to be enormous cloth backdrops on the stage, painted perhaps 20 or more years ago! They were, in fact, quite well done, but not what I had in mind. Nevertheless, the building itself was interesting, as were the old town photographs hanging on the walls. One could easily see that not all that much had changed in Irasburg in the past hundred years.

Upon exiting the Town Hall, I spied a sign at the far end of the common which read "Historic Irasburg." Here I found not only history, but comedy as well. According to the sign, it seems that Ira Allen, after whom the town was named, was given the entire locale in 1786 as payment for his surveying services. Twelve years later in 1798, along came Caleb Leach, who arrived "carrying all of his belongings in a handsled." Being the first settler, he was given half the town for free. ( I had to assume that Mr. Allen probably had not actually lived in town.) Two years later, the Sylvester family moved in. They were squatters and knew nothing of the other fellow until they bumped into him. Three years later, the first town meeting was held – you can guess who the two selectmen were and also wonder who was there to vote. In the end, it seems the surveyor, the sledman and the squatter all made out pretty well for themselves, once again proving that the early bird catches the worm.

But all were not so fortunate in Irasburg. Still to come were the flood, the fire and the "Irasburg affair." The flood struck in November of 1927 and, according to the sign, "the home of Arie and Myra Kennison was swept off its foundation and floated downriver. The family had warning and were able to save their cow... their house was recovered and relocated farther away from the river." The fire broke out in July of 1936, destroying 10 houses and four businesses.

Most recently, the "Irasburg affair" shook up the town. This involved the Reverend David Johnson, an unemployed black minister who had moved here with his family and a white houseguest with two children. In the summer of 1968, a carload of young people drove by the house shouting and shooting. The state police were stationed at the house for several weeks to protect the family, but "the only result of their occupation was the arrest of Reverend Johnson for adultery with his houseguest, Barbara Lawrence." The Johnsons soon returned to California. Such is the history of Irasburg.

Follow State Route 58 east through Orleans. Just past Evansville, you will see a sign for **Brownington Center** and the **Old Stone House Museum**, built in the 1830s. Formerly a school house, the four-story building displays colonial household items.

Continue on State Route 58 for another 10 minutes or so and take a right onto State Route 5A heading south. As you descend on this road, **Lake Willoughby** emerges in all its dramatic glory. If you have never seen the lake, you are in for a pleasant surprise. With its long slender shape flanked on two sides by steep rock-faced cliffs that plummet almost directly to the water itself, this is a lake to be remembered. Certainly, there are no others quite like it in Vermont. Continue on State Route 5A and drive along the eastern shore to the southern end of the lake. Though you will most likely want to stare out the window across the water, beware – there is little room for error on this narrow lake road.

Once at the south end, there is a small parking lot. It's a good place to get out of the car, stretch and walk along the water's edge. As you face the lake, the mountain to your right is the 2,751-foot Mount Pisgah, part of the **Willoughby State Forest**, which offers camping and hiking.

Retrace your drive back north along the five-mile lake road and take a left onto State Route 16. Here, at the northern tip of the lake, there is a much larger beach and parking lot. Keep it in mind if you are here in the summer that the water is especially clear.

# Barton

Rolling, open fields accented with casually placed masses of evergreens greet the eye as you make your way to Barton. Just before the town center, look for the signpost (minus the sign) on your left which marks the entrance to **Crystal Lake State Park**. Unfortunately, like many other northern state parks, it is closed for the winter, but you can park briefly near the gate or in town and walk in. It's a nice spot with a spacious green lawn and a sandy beach. Like Lake Willoughby, is 'crystal' clear – thus, aptly named.

For small towns, Barton center can be fairly tricky. In my haste to pass through the jumble of streets, I took a wrong turn and ended up heading back north to Orleans instead of south on State Route 16. Fortunately for me, I turned around and headed back into Barton, where I decided to take a closer look at this unique town. What I found was one of the most visually exciting towns I had seen in a long time. The autumn sun was low and golden, creating fabulous patterns of warm brilliant light and cool shadows upon the old houses which rise and fall dramatically in this town of hills. I spent the next hour walking and driving, picking out some good painting spots. I could hardly wait to see it in winter as well. I was glad I had taken that wrong turn!

# Glover

Back on State Route 16 heading south, take a left turn onto State Route 122 and go a half-mile to Glover and the headquarters of the **Bread and Puppet Theater**. You can't miss the many brightly painted barns that house the museum. Inside, huge puppets, masks, posters and other paraphernalia can be viewed. The annual summer circus presented by the theater is held every year on a nearby field, bringing thousands of fans from far and wide.

Enjoy the remaining stretch of scenic State Route 16, which will bring you directly back into Hardwick.

## For More Information
*(Area code 802 unless noted otherwise)*

| | |
|---|---|
| Bread and Puppet Theater Museum | ☎ 525-3031 |
| Craftsbury Center | ☎ 800-729-7751 |
| Crystal Lake State Park | ☎ 525-6205 |
| Hardwick Chamber of Commerce | ☎ 472-5906 |
| Old Stone House Museum | ☎ 754-2022 |
| Northeast Kingdom Chamber of Commerce | ☎ 800-639-6379 |
| Northeast Kingdom Fall Foliage Festival | ☎ 563-2472 |

## For Accommodations
*(Area code 802 unless noted otherwise)*

**In Irasburg**
| | |
|---|---|
| Brick House Bed and Breakfast | ☎ 754-2108 |

**In Orleans**
| | |
|---|---|
| Green Acres Cabins | ☎ 525-3722 |

**In Greensboro**
| | |
|---|---|
| Highland Lodge | ☎ 533-2647 |

**In Craftsbury Common**
    Inn on the Common               ☎ 800-521-2233
**In Westmore**
    Willough Vale Inn and Restaurant    ☎ 800-541-0588

# Chapter 5

# New Hampshire

# Along the Connecticut River

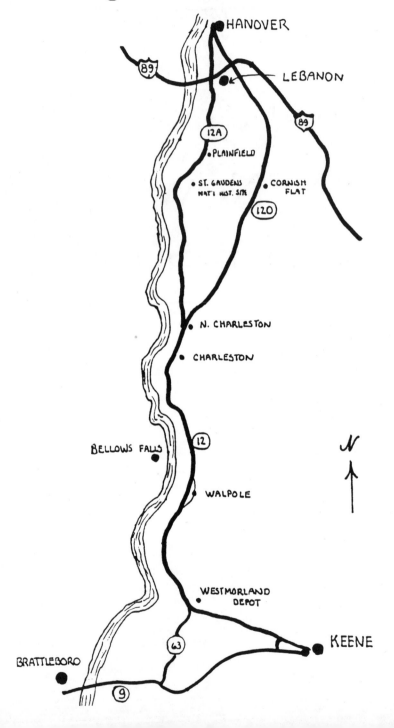

# Along The Connecticut River, Southern New Hampshire

 For this tour, leave Interstate 91 at exit 3 in Brattleboro, Vermont. Head east on State Route 9 for seven miles into New Hampshire. Take State Route 63 north, which intersects State Route 12 at Westmoreland. The tour begins here and ends in Hanover and can be done in one day. The peak foliage is expected from October 11th to 18th.

> **Highlights:** *Connecticut River, historic towns, pumpkin patches, antique shops, cheese-making plant, historic sites, foliage train ride, longest covered bridge in U.S., Bellows Falls, colonial fortification replica, Saint-Gaudens historic site, towns of Walpole and Hanover.*

River routes have a unique character all of their own. The mountains that we are used to in this area of Vermont and New Hampshire tend to fade into the background, while valleys and fields create a natural highway on a grand scale. The distances and views here are not seen from mountain tops, but rather from across meadows, and, perhaps most beautiful of all, from the river's edge. Whether we gaze up, down, or across this magnificent New England river, there is a heightened sense of poetry, as with any great natural feature. And its poetry is not diminished by season or weather. Even time and the encroachment of modern man has not destroyed the beauty of the Connecticut

River, which provides the boundary between Vermont and New Hampshire and is perhaps in its most natural state here.

Generally speaking, the foliage along rivers tends to turn and peak a week or so later than the surrounding higher altitudes, leaving quite a bit of green along the river while it is peak season in the outlying areas. There are plenty of maples, but they are not as dominant as in other parts of the state. The mixture of evergreens, oaks, birches, beech, box elder and the occasional willow gives this area a slightly more subdued coloring.

# Westmoreland Depot

Beginning our river ramble on New Hampshire State Route 12 in Westmoreland Depot, your first stop might be the **Aching Acres Farm**, just north of here in Walpole. If you are a pumpkin lover, and especially if you have young children with you, then you won't want to miss this farm. Besides wandering through the pumpkin patch, where you can pick your own, there is a petting zoo to visit, a glass beehive observatory and a small red schoolhouse where classic fairy tales are told in the Story Book Village. On weekends, demonstrations show skills such as extracting honey, making beeswax candles, processing gourds and carving pumpkins.

# Walpole

The entire route along State Route 12 is a nice drive and you may not want to get off, but you would be making a big mistake if you missed the beautiful and historic town of Walpole. Take a right turn onto South Road, where you will see a sign for the Walpole business district. There are two good antique shops immediately to your right at the bend in the road. Stop in and say hello to Judy Boynton at the **Golden Past Antiques**. She's been in the business a long time and has the enthusiasm and knowledge it takes. Watch out for her little dog, who may be underfoot. I had the scare of my life when I accidently stepped on the little shaver and he let out a yelp that almost sent me through the roof.

One minute farther up South Road, you will enter Walpole center, founded in 1752. Grand homes and buildings greet you on Main Street, some of which have been occupied by well-known individuals. The **Academy Building** was constructed in 1831 and now belongs to the Walpole Historical Society, which offers a foliage tour brochure. Make sure you pick up one if you are interested in doing some further exploration. Also on Main Street is the **River Valley Fine Arts Gallery**, which includes the works of five or six fine contemporary New England artists.

Take a left at the fountain on Main Street and make your way around the old town common, lined by beautiful homes as well as two churches. It is a good place to walk and stretch before heading onward – and a spot you won't forget.

# Drewsville

Before leaving the area, you may want to head up the old Drewsville Road just north of town. You will pass by the **Flint grave**, the exact spot where Thomas Flint and his companion were ambushed and killed by Indians in 1755 while they were out gathering wood. Farther along, cross Walpole Valley Road, turn right on State Route 123 and go to Drewsville for a glimpse of another, albeit smaller, old town common. The Walpole Valley Road also has the Dodge Tavern and the old Slade Cemetery.

To return to State Route 12, head out of Walpole on Main Street and bear left. To your right is **Mill Pond**, a wildlife refuge with nature trails.

The **Boggy Meadow Farm**, off River Road in Walpole, is of interest, being New Hampshire's first large-scale commercial producer of cheese. From inside the farm's cheese shop, visitors can look through a window into the plant to see how the cheese is made.

As you drive north on State Route 12, there is a small, hard-to-see stone marker on your right which marks the site of **John Kilburn's 1749 cabin**. He was the first settler in Walpole. According to the marker, "Here occurred his heroic defense against the Indians August 17, 1755."

Not more than a mile north of this marker is yet another, this time on the left. It marks the site of the **first Connecticut River bridge**, erected in 1785. A replacement was built in 1840 and was recognized in its day for its unique engineering style.

# Bellows Falls

An excellent detour off State Route 12 is just ahead at the traffic lights. Watch for the sign to Bellows Falls and the Railroad Station. Take a left here and cross over the Connecticut River falls and gorge. This used to be a great fishing place for Native American tribes, who were after the shad and Atlantic salmon that migrated up the river to spawn. In fact, if you know where to look, there are Indian petroglyphs carved on the rocks below. The carvings have apparently been retouched over the years and perhaps even outlined with paint a number of times in order not to lose them to erosion.

So that boats could avoid the falls, the **Bellows Falls Canal**, one of the first canals in the United States, was built and completed in 1802. In Bellows Falls the canal runs through the east side of town and you can pass over it on both Bridge and Depot Streets.

After crossing over the river, follow the signs to the **Railroad Station**. Here you can catch a ride on the *Green Mountain Flyer*. There are several different rides, but one of the most interesting is the **Fall Foliage Ride**, a 54-mile round-trip on a fully restored vintage passenger train. The train travels from Bellows Falls to Ludlow, Vermont and takes six hours. There is another interesting and shorter route to Chester Depot, Vermont. This ride is 26 miles long and takes two hours. I would strongly suggest reservations for either.

Back on State Route 12 in New Hampshire, the road becomes sandwiched between the river and the railroad tracks. This is a particularly nice stretch with river views looking across to Vermont. There are actually places to pull off the road and enjoy the scenery.

# Charlestown

The town of Charlestown emerges as we continue our trip north. Here, there is a stone marker at the original site where the town fortification was built in the early 1700s. The fort was attacked in 1747 by the French and Indians who were finally beaten off after a three-day battle.

After passing a wonderful and seemingly endless cornfield, you will see a sign on your left for Patch Park and for the **Fort at No.4**. Here, along the banks of the river, stands a life-size replica of the original fort of Charlestown. It is really a sight to see – and an unexpected one too. I had passed by here many times and never knew it existed. The fort is impressive, with high palisade walls and authenticity. One can go right down to the river's edge at the park to enjoy the beach and the large grass lawn for a bit of relaxation. The fort itself is open only through Columbus Day, but don't let that stop you from visiting. It's just as impressive from the outside and you can easily see through the palisade walls.

North of town the road forks. Bear left onto State Route 12A and continue to follow the river (and to avoid Claremont, which can be fairly congested and confusing). Travel a mile or so up to the small **North Charlestown** center. Look for the **1889 Farwell stone school** on your left. This is a real beauty and I was happy to see it had not only been well restored but that it was still being used as a school. Even the small modern addition was tasteful. The sprawling apple orchard immediately behind the building must provide a quick snack for hungry students. The school and the setting reminded me of the old stone one-room schoolhouse where I did my student teaching years ago in Devon, England. I well remember the day cows escaped from a nearby farm and poured into the schoolyard during recess, sending the little uniformed scholars screaming in all directions. I'm not sure who was more scared, the children, the cows, or the teacher!

# Cornish

When you reach the Cornish area, you can't miss the **Cornish-Windsor covered bridge**. If you think it is a long one, you are right. As you will see written on the sign, it is the "Longest wooden bridge in the U.S. and the longest two-span covered bridge in the world." It was built originally as a toll bridge in 1866 for $9,000. Naturally, I wanted to walk the 460-foot bridge, but unforunately there is no walking plank and the traffic is heavy. In fact, the two lanes of cars just manage to squeeze through.

A short distance ahead, past some nice river views and cornfields, there is a road on your right which leads to the Saint-Gaudens National Historic Site. The road is well marked. If you haven't visited here before, do yourself a favor and go.

**The Saint-Gaudens National Historic Site** is the former home, studio, grounds and gardens of the famous American sculptor Augustus Saint-Gaudens (1848-1907). Saint-Gaudens' arrival here in 1885 marked the beginning of The Cornish Colony, a group of artists that included the painters George de Forest Brush, Thomas Dewing, Stephen and Maxfield Parrish and Willard Metcalf. Scores of writers, poets, playwrights and musicians were soon to follow, many residing here only in the summer.

Among Saint-Gaudens' better known statues are those of Farra-gut (Madison Square, New York City), Sherman (also in New York on Fifth Avenue near Central Park), the Standing Lincoln, the Puritan and the Adams Memorial (Rock Creek Cemetery in Washington, D.C.). The latter, in my opinion, is one of the most moving. It is also one of the simplest. Depicting a seated woman in drapery, it was created as a memorial for the wife of Henry Adams. A duplicate of it, along with the others, is here on the grounds.

At the request of President Theodore Roosevelt, Saint-Gaudens also redesigned the $10 and $20 gold pieces. The rough plaster models and sketches for these beautiful coins are also on display.

The grounds surrounding the home provide a fabulous place to enjoy an hour or more outdoors. You don't need to be an artist to appreciate the landscape, gardens and trails that abound on the property. There is a view of Mount Ascutney across the spacious green lawn. Six-foot-high hedges enclose the gardens and in front of the house is the largest honey-locust tree in the state of New Hampshire, planted by the sculptor himself.

Back on State Route 12A heading north, watch for the little **Blow Me Down Mill**, built in 1891 alongside the small waterfall. There is a small parking area and a marker commemorating the Cornish Colony. President Woodrow Wilson spent several summers here in Cornish at the home of American author Winston Churchill. The house, which was just up the road from here, burned down in 1923.

When you reach Townline Farm Equipment in **Plainfield**, take a left onto Ferry Hill Road. The road begins through thick woodlands and an area of private homes but soon will bring you within yards of the Connecticut River. If you would like to explore some of the riverbank on foot and take in some fine views in three directions, including a river's edge view of Mount Ascutney, then this is the place to be. It is a fairly remote area with little traffic. You may also notice small signs designating the **Plainfield Wildflower Sanctuary**, which covers the hillside embankment opposite the river. Stay on this road and it will bring you back onto State Route 12A just north of Plainfield.

As you travel the next two or so miles toward Lebanon, you may begin to sense the approaching development ahead. The remaining beautiful cornfields seem to have their days sadly numbered. If you pass the Friendly's Restaurant on your left, you will have passed the point of no return of open spaces. Either succumb to the lure of fast food and shopping malls or keep your eyes straight ahead and drive onward. You can escape this by getting on Interstate 89, which will soon connect you with Interstate 91. Alternatively, stay on State Route 12A for another 10 miles and it will bring you directly into downtown Hanover.

# Hanover

Hanover may be the town you choose for your home base while on the road, as the journey described in this chapter could easily be traveled in reverse, or you may just want to give it a quick glance. Whatever your personal preference, the town is full of things to do. Being home of Dartmouth College, it has a unique character of its own.

Aside from the beauty of the campus and town itself, other attractions include the Hopkins Center for the Performing Arts, with concerts, plays, films and an art gallery, and the Hood Museum of Art, right next door. History buffs can visit the Hanover Historical Society Museum on North Main Street and book lovers can get lost in the maze of rooms that make up The Dartmouth Bookstore. The Hanover area has many hiking opportunities as well, including the **Appalachian Trail**. Information is available from the Dartmouth Outing Club or The Hanover Trails Association.

# For More Information
*(Area code 603 unless noted otherwise)*

| | |
|---|---|
| Aching Acres Farm | ☎ 756-4803 |
| Boggy Meadow Farm | ☎ 756-4874 |
| Dartmouth Outing Club | ☎ 646-2428 |
| The Fort at No.4 | ☎ 826-5700 |
| Green Mountain Railroad | ☎ 463-3069 |
| Hanover Trails Association | ☎ 643-2400 |
| Plainfield Wildflower Sanctuary | ☎ 617-877-7630 |
| River Valley Fine Arts | ☎ 756-4311 |
| Saint-Gaudens National Historic Site | ☎ 675-2175 |

# For Accommodations
*(Area code 603 unless noted otherwise)*

**In Cornish**

| | |
|---|---|
| Chase House Bed and Breakfast | ☎ 675-5391 |

**In West Lebanon**

| | |
|---|---|
| Airport Economy Inn | ☎ 800-433-3466 |

**In Hanover**

| | |
|---|---|
| The Hanover Inn | ☎ 800-443-7024 |
| Chiefton Motor Inn | ☎ 800-845-3557 |

# Monadnock Region, Southern New Hampshire

 To reach this region from Interstate 91, take exit 3 in Brattleboro, Vermont, and head east on State Route 9 to Keene. Watch for signs to State Route 101. The tour begins here, heading east out of Keene and returns to Keene. This trip can be made in one day. The peak foliage is expected from October 5th to 11th.

> **Highlights:** *Mount Monadnock views and hiking, Pack Monadnock, historic towns, excellent bookstores, woodland hiking trails, apple picking, ponds and bogs, Peterborough, Jaffery, Harrisville, Hancock, marionette theater and art galleries.*

Think of Southern New Hampshire and autumn and it is most likely you will think of the Monadnock region. The reasons may be many, from the classic old New England towns to the lure of the mighty **Mount Monadnock**. Rich in ponds, bogs, trails, gleaming white colonial homes and full of culture, the area has been a magnet to many. But it is the mountain, in fact, which takes top billing.

What a time of year to see this southern giant which may very well welcome more visitors, both young and old, than any other mountain in the United States. If ever there were a people's mountain, approachable and welcoming (except in the dead of winter) and beloved by so many, this would be it. In spite of the millions of booted feet that have climbed it over the last three centuries, it still retains its simple beauty, grandeur and dignity as most great things do. Thoreau, one of many well-known figures to visit this area and hike the mountain, spoke of the power it has over those who climb about its flanks, a certain life force to be reckoned with. I climbed this mountain several times as a boy and to this day vividly recall the sensation, especially as I hopped and jumped about the high summit boulders. Rock, sky, clouds and a wind to carry you aloft and soaring is what I remember most. These essential elements of nature and little else, unchanged for millions of years, are the ingredients for a powerful experience.

# Monadnock Region

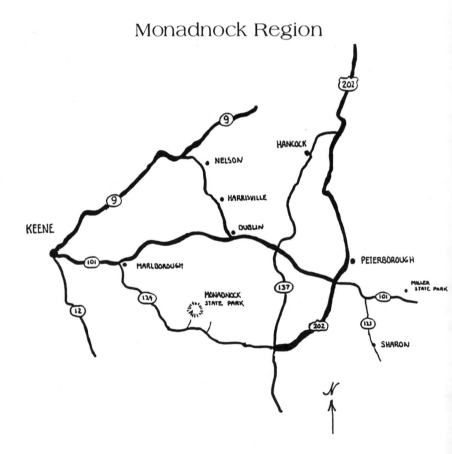

The surrounding Monadnock towns, such as Jaffery, Peterborough, Hancock and Dublin, have their own individual draw and cast a spell on thousands of visitors every year. The fact that more than a handful of people choose to live here while commuting to Boston daily to work speaks for itself.

If you decide to climb the mountain and take the time to explore and enjoy the surrounding towns, parks and shops, then you could easily spend two or three days here – I would recommend that. The route described in this chapter, however, can be driven in a matter of hours. But who can resist an autumn hike, a beckoning dirt road, an old town library, a picnic by the pond, or a good bookstore?

# Keene

Although this tour does not include all that Keene has to offer, you may be interested in the **Stonewall Farm** off Chesterfield Road. The farm features a hayride, children's corn maze, farm animals and a large pumpkin patch. In addition, call the Keene Chamber of Commerce to find out about the **Harvest Festival** held downtown.

State Route 101 is easily picked up from Keene's Main Street or State Route 9. Traveling east, it is three miles to the town of **Marlborough**. Here, book lovers will enjoy **The Homestead Bookshop**, just beyond the village. Beware, there are over 45,000 rare and used books in this old farm building.

# Jaffrey

Follow the sign for State Route 124 south toward Jaffrey. After passing the Frost Free Library and going up and down a few hills, you will have your first sight of Mount Monadnock. It is only a teaser though, as there are even better views to come. Soon, you will arrive at a beautiful pond that spreads on both sides of the road. Places like this are stunning in autumn, as the warm orange of the foliage contrasting against the deepest of blue skies echoes on the surface of the still water.

Not more than a mile beyond this, you will reach one of several entrances to the mountain trails. From here, you can park the car and hike up **Mount Monadnock** on the Old Toll Road, which will lead you to the Halfway House site. From there, you can pick up the White Arrow Trail, one of the 12 trails leading to the summit. If these names mean nothing to you, there is a good trail map, available from the rangers, giving distances and levels of difficulty.

If you'd like to visit the **Mount Monadnock State Park** headquarters, just keep driving on State Route 124 about a mile more. Follow the State Park signs, making a left turn off the main road. Here, you will find the visitors center, a picnic area, a refreshment stand and restrooms. You may also find bus-loads of school children arriving to climb the mountain. This is usually where most large groups come, due to the access to the easier trails and the public facilities. And by the looks of these students, a good climb should be just what the doctor ordered.

If you climb to the 3,165-foot summit of this mountain, termed "the new Olympus" by Ralph Waldo Emerson, you will be rewarded with a hundred-mile panoramic view in all directions. On a clear day, some part of six states can be seen. The White Dot Trail, which begins at the parking lot, is certainly one of the more popular, being the shortest and most direct route to the summit. But whatever trail you decide to take, remember the journey along the way is half the fun.

Henry David Thoreau visited here twice in 1858 and again in 1860, camping for a week along the Amphitheater Trail and the White Cross Trail. You will do well to remember his words, quoted in the visitors center, "It is remarkable what haste the visitors make to get to the top of the mountain and then look away from it... the great charm is not to look off from a height but to walk over this novel and wonderful surface."

On exiting the park, take a left instead of a right turn for a scenic detour. A minute's drive will bring you to the **Gilson Road** on your right. Follow this for some wonderful views looking back across a pond and marsh towards the mountain. There are a couple of nice homes here with backyard views made in heaven. The Gilson Road will soon intersect with the Thorndike Pond Road. By taking a right here, you will meet up again with State Route 124. On this road, you will see some classic 19th-century homes which anyone would be proud to own, as well as the **1833 Melville Academy Building**.

The understated historical splendor of downtown Jaffery emerges just before the junction of State Route 124 and 137. The **Jaffrey Civic Center**, housing the Historical Society, will be on your left. Next to it is the old red brick **Clay Library**. Both buildings, looking quite smart, are set back from the street across an expanse of deep green lawns sprinkled with fallen yellow leaves. Unfortunately, these buildings have very limited hours, so it is best to call the Chamber of Commerce before your visit if you are interested.

Directly across the street from the Civic Center is th**e Cutler Memorial Building** and a former church, built in 1844. The handsome exterior caught my interest and curiosity, so I walked through the open doors to get a look inside. It was clear that the nicely renovated interior was no longer meant for worship. According to the friendly woman inside who was busy organizing an upcoming rummage sale, the building is now run by the Women's Club. Thanks to them, the old, crumbling steeple was recently restored. The town, however, still owns the clock. Both are to be admired and remembered!

Leaving Jaffrey, take a left onto State Route 137 north towards Hancock. After a few miles of woodland, the road suddenly opens up for a refreshing view across a grassy bog. There are a few places to pull off the road and eat your apple. Continue straight ahead, through the intersection of State Route 101 and into the historic town of Hancock. Now here's a little town with a big punch.

# Hancock

Typical of old New England, the quiet and gentle simplicity rarely reveal the extraordinary history and secrets within. I'm convinced you could chose any one of these towns to research, no matter how small, and be pleasantly surprised by the hidden facts you discover. One piece of information usually leads to another and it can quickly become an historical obsession, much to the dismay of those left at home. Fortunately for me, Mike (my brother and co-author) is the one with the family and I can spend the extra day or two on research if I need the time. And I did. Hancock was only one of many towns where my planned brief visit turned into days of poking about.

Every building on Hancock's Main Street has been entered in the National Register of Historic Places and the first one you are likely to see is the **First Congregational Church**. It's a real beauty, built in 1788 across the street from its present location and moved in 1851. Apparently building-moving happened rather frequently in the old days – sometimes even entire towns were moved.

Next to the church is the post office and behind it, the **Norway Pond Beach**, named after the few remaining Norway pines around the shore. This is a good spot for a lunch break or at least another apple.

Across the road from the pond is the **Pine Ridge Cemetery** with graves dating back to the early 1800s. There's nothing like a stroll through a graveyard to give you a good healthy perspective on life. Reading old tombstones can be engrossing. Many have the epitaph of the day, but occasionally you stumble across an original, such as on the tomb of Dorcas Freeman who died in

1900. It simply states, "She hath done what she could." It kind of made me wonder... what did she do?

Try to find the grave of Benjamin Ball. It appears as if Benjamin is buried in someone else's tomb. While his name appears on the door, above the door the words "Sybel Ball's Tomb" are engraved. On studying the rest of the nearby Ball family tombstones, you'll see the tomb of Sybbel (sic) Ball who died in 1873, some 35 years after Benjamin. Had Sybel been the wife of Benjamin it might make some sense that she purchased the tomb for her and her husband. It could be that the daughter Sybel purchased her father's tomb. But why would she have her own name carved so boldly? At the real grave of Sybel, the name is spelled with two b's, while the other is spelled with one. Is it the same Sybel? And if you study further, you'll find that Benjamin was married to Mary. Look also at the grave of Betsy. Her name has been spelled with an extra "s" on the end, reading, "Betsy Balls daughter of Mary and Benjamin Balls." It all makes you wonder if the epitaph on Jonas Ball's tombstone isn't an angry message meant for the careless engraver – "Meet me in Heaven."

New Hampshire's oldest continually operating inn, the **Hancock Inn**, is just down the road on Main Street. I was graciously given a tour of this beautiful building, which has been offering accommodations and meals to travelers since 1789, George Washington's first year as president. The inn has been restored with period fabrics, furniture and antiques. I got the distinct feeling as I toured many of the bedrooms, all different, that I had stepped back two hundred years.

One of the bedrooms, the Rufus Porter room, is of particular interest. The walls retain the eloquent murals of painter Rufus Porter (1792 to 1884), known to some as America's most versatile and productive itinerant. Something of a jack-of-all-trades, Porter painted murals in exchange for free lodging. His work can be found throughout New Hampshire, southern Maine and northern Massachusetts.

Later, as I browsed the town library, a small painting of a young girl caught my eye. The quality of the work drew me nearer for a closer inspection. This is how I discovered Lilla Cabot Perry's connection with the town of Hancock. As a painter of landscapes, figures and sometimes portraits, she studied with the Boston painters Dennis Miller Bunker and Robert Vonnoh. In 1889, she traveled to France to meet Monet and paint at Giverny. Later, in 1903, she purchased a farmhouse in Hancock along with 250 acres. At first it was only a summer retreat, but as the years passed, she began spending more time here, painting what Monet encouraged her to paint – the landscape.

After your visit in Hancock, head up the Norway Hill Road near the end of Main Street to the **Norway Hill Orchard**. The orchard is a good place to pick up to five varieties of apples. It is open until late October.

Also in Hancock, off Kings Highway, is the **Harris Center for Conservation Education**. Here, several looping trails travel through 4,000 acres of unspoiled woodlands. There's no charge and you can enjoy one of the many guided tour programs as well as hike on your own.

The Norway Hill Road will take you directly to State Route 202. Take a right onto State Route 202 west (which actually goes south) toward Peterborough.

# Peterborough

Rich in history, culture, natural resources and beauty, Peterborough is a place you'll want to visit more than once. The town, visited by Thornton Wilder in the 1930s, inspired him to write *Our Town*. Peterborough also boasts the first public library in the world that a town, in 1833, voted to fund. The MacDowell Colony, a unique short-term residential village for all types of artists, is also located here. Wilder spent 10 summers at the Colony, along with many other well-known figures.

As you travel down State Route 202, take a right onto State Route 101 west. Immediately on your right you will see the chamber of commerce, a good place to stop for information if you are spending any time in the area. Just beyond the chamber, take a right onto Grove Street. This will lead you into the heart of downtown Peterborough. The thriving town is well worth exploring, whatever your interests.

There are two antique shops across from one another on Grove Street, as well as the **Parchment and Plate Book Store**, which features old books. If you have any interest in art, do not miss **Peter Pelletier Fine Art**, at 32 Grove Street. I was thrilled to have come across the gallery quite by accident. I visited for over an hour admiring the quality early 20th-century paintings and speaking with Peter, whom I found to be friendly and knowledgable about this subject.

Just around the corner on Main Street is the unique **New England Marionette Opera**, America's largest marionette theater devoted primarily to opera. Ask at the ticket office about their upcoming performances (on weekends only) and if you may take a peek at the theater itself. The handmade puppets are painted and costumed in the shop and are brought to life by the dozen skilled manipulators, who work 11 feet above the stage.

One of the area's largest and most popular bookstores is just a minute's walk from the theater on Depot Street. **Toadstool Bookshop** features over 40,000 books along with a small café. I walked in for a quick browse and the owners must have thought I wouldn't leave till the next day!

When you've had enough shop-hopping, you can visit the **Seccombe Nature Park**, adjacent to Adams Playground between Union Street and MacDowell Road. The park offers 22 acres of land laced with walking trails. If that doesn't suit you, head east on State Route 101 and watch for the sign on your left directing you to the **Sheiling Forest** off Old Street Road. The 45 acres of woodlands, given to the state by Mrs. Elizabeth McGreal, is open to the public at no charge. You can walk the Loop Trail in an hour or less. A guide is available to point out certain plants, trees and natural areas of interest.

A few miles farther on State Route 101, watch for the sign that directs you to the **Sharon Arts Center**, four miles down State Route 123 south. There's an exhibition gallery, small art library, a superb crafts gallery and a gift shop. On your way back to State Route 101, watch for the sign on your left for the **Upland Farm**, a great place to pick your own apples – 12 varieties of them!

Continue east on State Route 101 for 2½ miles to reach **Pack Monadnock Mountain** in Miller State Park. If you didn't have the opportunity to climb Mount Monadnock or were unable to for other reasons, then this is the place to go. At Pack Monadnock, you can actually drive up the 2,280-foot summit on a steep and twisting paved road. The charge is $2.50 per person and the drive takes under 10 minutes. The view from the top is fabulous and the larger Mount Monadnock can be seen clearly to the west. On a clear day, the Boston skyline is visible to the south and to the north is Mount Washington.

I had a nice chat with the good-natured ranger who was eager to share a wealth of information about the mountain. Established in 1891, the park is New Hampshire's oldest state park. Nineteen trails lead to the summit and the Marion Davis Trail, which begins here at the parking lot, is 1.4 miles. A variety of trees, including maple, oak, birch, mountain ash and beech, cover the mountain. Violets and asters are among the wildflowers found in season, along with the ever-popular blueberries.

The summit, according to the ranger, used to be open pasture for sheep. Now, except for the bald peak, the summit is surrounded by beautiful stunted and twisted oak trees and, unfortunately, a handful of communications towers. With the usual wind that prevails up there, it can be quite cold, even on a warm autumn day. Go prepared, even if you're driving to the top and plan to stay in your car.

One final note about the mountain... hawks, hawks and more hawks. In mid-September, the Audubon Society sponsors a **Hawk Watch**, which is open to the public. During this migration period, the hawks, mostly broad-winged and redtail, can be seen catching a ride on the winds and sailing about the summit. On a good day you can see hundreds or even thousands of them. I have to wonder how birders counts two thousand hawks flying overhead without counting the same one twice! Keep a sharp eye out for the eagles too.

# Dublin

Head back west on State Route 101 toward yet another noted elevation, Dublin. At 1,493 feet above sea level, it is known as the highest village in New England. You may not notice this altitude as you drive through the small town center. The several buildings in the town center on State Route 101 are an interesting and historic group. On your left will be the old Dublin Church, the 1882 Town Hall, an antique shop and the library, a one-of-a-kind stone treasure. Across the street in the large red building are the *Yankee Books* and *Yankee Magazine* headquarters. Speaking of books, there is the **Monadnock Books and Antiques** a little farther up on your right, located in Dublin's oldest house. Also in Dublin, off Goldmine Road, is the **Honey Lane Farm**, which offers horseback riding and lessons, excursions and lodging.

In order to get to Harrisville and Nelson, absolute must-sees if you enjoy small and unique old New England towns, take the right turn immediately after the Dublin firehouse and follow this road up past the Dublin school. There's a good view to your right not far from the school, confirming that Dublin is actually on higher ground. From here, the road twists and turns every which way to Harrisville.

# Harrisville

Certainly Harrisville would receive the "red brick building award" if there were one. Almost every structure in the historic center is made of red bricks, which makes for an unusual, though homogeneous, character. This is a town you must walk around, so shake a leg, grab your camera and explore. A National Historic Landmark, this town is beautiful from every angle.

Through the center of the town runs the **Nubanusit Brook**, which forms a small pond, acting somewhat like a town common made of water. From here, the water cascades in a series of waterfalls down the hill toward the south side of town. The historic red buildings reflected in the water along with the brilliant colors of the surrounding maples make this an extremely picturesque town. Side streets rise and fall in a glorious jumble radiating from the center.

Small as the town may be, giving directions is not so easy. It usually happens that whenever I arrive in a new town (anywhere in the world) someone inevitably approaches me within the first few minutes and asks for directions. The strange thing is I seem to be able to give them. Such was the case in Harrisville: an enormous delivery truck pulled up and asked me where such and such building was and, as I had just seen the sign, I was able to tell him. My record remained untarnished.

The town cemetery has a great location on what would probably be the choicest real estate in town. It's situated on a peninsula surrounded on three sides by the beautiful Harrisville Pond and open to anyone – though the prerequisite to this great spot makes the move a permanent one. For another view of the pond, there's a small town beach just off one of the side streets.

# Nelson

If you've come this far to visit Harrisville, I would suggest driving a few miles more along the main road and going to Nelson for a peek at a very small and sparse town center. There is a town green surrounded by the church, the library and the 1787 Town Hall, along with a few homes. Unlike Harrisville, with its many brick structures in a cluster, Nelson's attraction lies in its lack of buildings and the breadth of its design. There is a true quality of early colonial times here, undisturbed and quietly forgotten.

To return to the 20th century and to Keene, continue along Nelson's main road for another mile and you will run directly into State Route 9. Take a left (west) toward Keene.

## For More Information
*(Area code 603 unless noted otherwise)*

| | |
|---|---|
| Greater Keene Chamber of Commerce | ☎ 352-1303 |
| Greater Peterborough Chamber of Commerce | ☎ 924-7234 |
| Harris Center for Conservation Education | ☎ 525-3394 |
| The Homestead Bookshop | ☎ 876-4213 |
| Honey Lane Farm | ☎ 563-8364 |
| Miller State Park | ☎ 547-3497 |
| Monadnock Books and Antiques | ☎ 563-7055 |
| Monadnock State Park | ☎ 532-8862 |
| New England Marionette Opera | ☎ 924-4333 |
| Norway Hill Orchard | ☎ 525-4912 |
| Peter Pelletier Fine Art, Inc. | ☎ 924-7558 |
| Seccombe Nature Park | ☎ 924-6712 |
| Sharon Arts Center | ☎ 924-7256 |
| Stonewall Farm | ☎ 357-7278 |
| Toadstool Bookshop | ☎ 924-3543 |
| Upland Farm | ☎ 924-3163 |

# For Accommodations
## *(Area code 603)*

**In Jaffrey**
The Gould Farm Bed and Breakfast     ☎ 532-6996
Woodbound Inn     ☎ 532-8341
The Benjamin Prescott Inn     ☎ 532-6637
The Monadnock Inn     ☎ 532-7001
**In Hancock**
The Hancock Inn     ☎ 525-3318
**In Harrisville**
The Harrisville Squires' Inn     ☎ 827-3925
**In Peterborough**
Apple Gate Bed and Breakfast     ☎ 924-6543

# The Kancamagus Highway

 Take I-93 to exit 32 at Lincoln. Drive east onto State Route 112, the Kancamagus Highway. The 35-mile trip, including stops, can be done in a day. Peak foliage expected: October 8-15th.

**Highlights:** *Scenic overlooks, mountain views, brilliant foliage, hiking trails, cascading waterfalls, the beautiful Swift River and much more.*

Beginning at the East Branch of the Pemigewasset River in Lincoln, climbing 3,000 feet along the side of Mount Kancamagus and then following the banks of the Swift River as you head toward Conway, the Kancamagus Highway is a treasure trove of natural scenic wonders. Named after Chief Kancamagus (The Fearless One), who was the grandson of Passaconaway and was the last Sagamon of the Penacook Confederacy, the Kancamagus was recently designated a National Scenic Byway.

The highway is no secret to tourists, who flock to the White Mountains. At peak foliage season you will definitely not be alone. For this reason you may want to come a few weeks earlier. Remember too, that it's a great place in summer as well, especially if you like good swimming holes. No matter when you come, you should experience what the highway has to offer at least once, even if it means contending with a bit of traffic. The 34½-mile road can be driven in about 45 minutes without stopping, but to do so would cheat you of some of the very best views and the essence of this wilderness area. You will at least want to stop at the scenic overlooks provided. These areas allow for views both north and south. The Sugar Hill overlook has a good panoramic view with a diagram showing you exactly what you are looking at: Potash Mountain, The Three Sisters and bald peaked Mount Chocura are all in view.

Maples, hemlock, oak, beech and an abundance of birch trees surround the highway, some of them fairly old and gnarled. This gives the area a lot of character, the trees clinging to the rocky banks of the Swift. There are numerous places to stop and enjoy the river views, which rival any of the panoramic mountain views.

Traveling east of Lincoln, the **Loon Mountain Recreation Area** makes a nice stop for a picnic along the banks of the East Branch. I've been swimming here in the summer and the water is among the clearest I've seen anywhere. The **Loon Mountain Ski Resort** is just beyond and hosts an Oktoberfest and Fall Foliage Festival around the first of October. Call the numbers listed at the end of this chapter for more information.

## The Kancamagus Highway

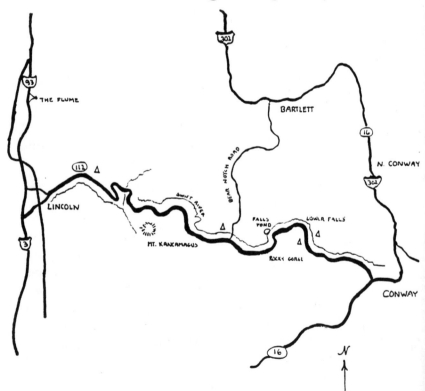

# Lincoln

Another mile up on the left look for the **Lincoln Woods Trail Center**. There is an information center here, restrooms and, most importantly, access to numerous hiking trails.

The **Otter Rocks** rest area is another nice spot along the river, although more intimate in setting. Just past here there is a series of scenic overlooks worth stopping at, especially if the weather is clear. Past the summit of Mt. Kancamagus, the road begins to descend and travels alongside the Swift River.

If you'd like to take a short hike and see a great waterfall, pull over into the **Sabbaday Falls** parking lot on your right. The walk to the falls takes about 10 minutes. The woods here are beautiful and the falls is actually a series of several falls carving out a small gorge and emptying into clear and very cold pools. The falls reportedly got its name from the early settlers who used to visit here on the Sabbath.

Should you be more ambitious when it comes to hiking, there are plenty of other trails that go on for miles. At the **Greeley Pond Scenic Area** for instance, you can pick up the Greeley Pond Trail, which will take you through some old-growth forest of spruce and fir, by some cliffs and on to the ponds.

If you don't want to hike, but would like to see more scenic vistas, then take the **Bear Notch Road** off to your left near the Jigger Johnson Campground. It's a nine-mile paved road with plenty of twists and turns and at least four good scenic overlooks. If you travel the entire length you will arrive at State Route 302.

Continuing east, the **Rocky Gorge Scenic Area** is also a good stop. Here, the river pours through a narrow gorge it has worn in the rocks. Cross the footbridge over the gorge and keep on a short distance to discover the beauty of **Falls Pond**. The river here is wonderful and you can walk along it for about a half-mile on the paved road from the parking lot.

An even more interesting stretch of river can be easily explored at the **Lower Falls Recreation Area**, three miles up the road. There is a large parking lot and restrooms are available. You can walk along the river on the huge boulders and explore the little waterfalls, rapids and pools. In summer this is a very popular swimming hole and definitely makes my Top Ten list. Be fore-warned – the rocks can be extremely slippery.

One of the last stops on the highway is **Champney Falls**. Named after the artist Benjamin Champney, the falls has a series of cascades about 70 feet long. It's a rather long hike, taking about 2½ hours, round trip.

Enjoy the last few blessed miles of the Kancamagus because the wonders of nature abruptly come to an end once you enter Conway. There are mobs of people here summer and fall and, unless you like traffic jams, you'll want to turn right around and head for the hills... again.

# For More Information
*(Area code 603)*

| | |
|---|---|
| Loon Mountain | ☎ 745-8111 |
| Loon Mountain Ski Resort | ☎ 745-6281, ext. 5530 |
| (Oktoberfest and Fall Foliage Festival) | |
| White Mountain National Forest, Conway | ☎ 447-5448 |
| Conway Village Chamber of Commerce | ☎ 447-2639 |
| White Mountains Attractions | ☎ 745-8720 |

# For Accommodations
*(Area code 603)*

| | |
|---|---|
| Conway Village Chamber of Commerce | ☎ 447-2639 |

# Chapter 6

# Maine

# Southern Maine

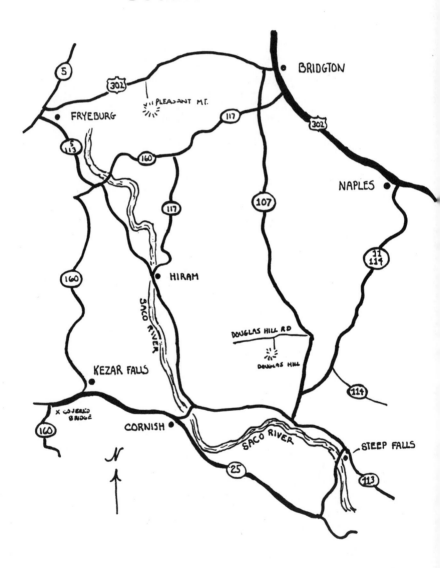

# Southern Maine Ramble

 For this tour, take exit 7 off Interstate 95 and follow Route 114 northwestward toward Sebago. When you reach Gorham, go west on Route 25. Stay on Route 25 through the center of Standish, then look for Route 113 north and turn here. Follow Route 113 to the village of Steep Falls in the township of Standish. Peak foliage is expected from early to mid-October.

**Highlights:** *Mountain tops, canoeing the Saco River, mountain gorge, museums, fall fairs, boat tours, covered bridges, colorful local history and more.*

The **Saco River** winds its way southeastward from the White Mountains of New Hampshire and through the rolling hills of southern Maine, traveling roughly 140 miles on its journey to the sea. Local Indians named the river Saco, which means "a snakelike stream running midst the pine trees." The description is quite accurate, but besides the tall white pines for which Maine is famous, maple, oak, beech and birch add to the rich colors blanketing the region each autumn. (Another interpretation of the Indian name is "outflowing," equally accurate for the giant watershed the river drains.)

Southern Maine is best known for sprawling Sebago Lake. That's fine with me as it keeps the country roads just west of the lake free of traffic. Here, you can poke along during a fall ramble and have plenty of elbow room. The countryside is more densely wooded than other sections of New England, with fewer farms opening up the panoramic views so common in Vermont. But if you know where to look and don't mind a few short hikes, the visual rewards can be spectacular. And if you love to canoe or have always wanted to try, the Saco River is a perfect waterway to explore while enjoying fall's colors from a new perspective.

# Standish & Sebago

Our ramble begins at Steep Falls on the Saco River in the town of Standish. At the junction of Route 113 and Route 11, take Route 11 south and you will reach the river in less than half a mile. Park on the right side of the bridge before the river at a small dirt pull-off.

At various points in time, the rushing water at Steep Falls powered mills, but little is left of these structures as nature has taken over. Upstream from the parking area, the shoreline is sandy, a perfect place to picnic while listening to the sound of the water. A foot trail leads to the very edge of the six-foot falls passing by water-worn rock formations.

Just above the falls, the river is entirely framed by trees, many of them swamp maples (red maples), which turn crimson in the early autumn.

For a mountain-top view of the area visit **Douglas Mountain**, a few minutes' drive to the north. Follow Route 11 north, then bear left onto Route 107 north. After five miles, look for Douglas Hill Road on the left and turn here, then take another quick left onto Douglas Mountain Road, which goes to the base of the mountain.

The walk to the summit on the Ledges Trail is a steep but short quarter-mile climb that passes beneath a forest of hemlock, pine, birch, beech, maple and striped maple. Ground cover includes mayflowers, blackberries, bracken ferns, goldenrod and various grasses. Closer to the top are red spruce and quaking aspen, sometimes called popple. In the open areas of ledges, low-bush blueberries can be identified by their scarlet leaves growing among the green juniper in the autumn. Quartz, feldspar and tourmaline can be seen in the ledges of brownish-gray schist.

The summit can also be reached via the Woods Trail, which is a bit longer but more gentle and can be negotiated even in winter.

At the summit you will see a large boulder, an erratic left by the retreating glaciers, with an inscription that reads "Non sibi sed omnibus," which means "not for one but for all." We are lucky the mountain is open to all of us and has been saved from development, thanks to the efforts of The Nature Conservancy, who purchased the 169-acre preserve in 1971.

The mountain was named for the Douglas brothers who settled here in the 1830s. Like many of New England's mountain tops, this one offers a hotel on its summit, named the **Douglas Inn**. It was built in the 1880s and attracted tourists, writers, artists and scholars, who all enjoyed the crisp air and inspiration given by the commanding views. At that time, the mountain and the surrounding hills were cleared for pasture, a vista far different than today's woodland scene.

A 16-foot stone tower was erected at the summit just before the hotel burned in 1928. Today, visitors can climb the tower and look out on the surrounding region. Mount Washington and the White Mountains can be seen to the northwest and, to the east, there is a nice view of Sebago Lake and other bodies of water. On especially clear days, the Atlantic Ocean is visible. The mountain is the highest point of land for several hundred square miles. For those who love fall's explosion of colors, this is the place to be.

After exploring Douglas Mountain, stop at the **Jones Museum**, also on Douglas Mountain Road. The museum exhibits glass and ceramic decorative art from all over the world and periodic programs feature expert collectors and artists.

Sebago Lake is just five miles east of Douglas Mountain and can be reached by getting back on Route 107, traveling south for about a mile, then turning left onto Long Hill Road. At the end of Long Hill Road, go left on Route 11/114, which follows the western shore of the lake northward. **Sebago Lake State Park** sits at the northern end of the lake and offers fishing, boating, hiking and picnicking. The Songo River winds through the park, adding to its beauty.

The **Songo River Queen II** offers daily tours during the summer and on weekends in September. One cruise takes you the length of the Songo River, through the historic Songo River Lock, built in 1830, to Sebago Lake and back, while another goes to Long Lake. The boat is on the bay at the Naples Causeway. **Naples** also makes a good stop for lunch or shopping, with restaurants, shops and other attractions. **Naples Flying Service** offers scenic seaplane rides from the lake, by appointment.

# Bridgton

The town of Bridgton is just a few miles north on Route 302. It, too, has shops and restaurants and anglers may want to stop in at the **Bait and Bucket** on Route 302 to ask where the fish are biting. The region is loaded with lakes and ponds that have fine smallmouth bass, largemouth bass and trout fishing. In Maine, almost every body of water smaller than Sebago is called a pond, including 10-mile long Moose Pond, where the state record largemouth was caught. I've enjoyed some fine fishing there, as well as on Tricky Pond, Peabody Pond and Kezar Pond.

The smallmouth bass just might be the strongest freshwater fish around. Once hooked, it makes powerful runs then usually catapults into the air, often shaking free. Autumn is a great time for smallmouth fishing – there are fewer boats and the fish are active. This is also a great period for trout fishing, as the fish move out of the deep holes and begin to feed closer to the surface.

In **South Bridgton**, off Ingals Road, the **Peabody-Fitch Farm**, also known by the Indian name "Narramissic," is a 1797 historic landmark. The farmstead includes a carriage house, barn and blacksmith shop. The property is owned by the Bridgton Historical Society, which also maintains a small museum on Gibbs Avenue near the center of Bridgton.

As you travel west out of Bridgton on Route 302, there is a nice view of Pleasant Mountain from the bridge over Moose Pond. Hikers can climb this mountain or try Jockey Cap or Starks Mountain farther down the road in Fryeburg.

# Fryeburg

During the first week of October each year, Fryeburg is host to the popular **Fryeburg Fair**. This agricultural fair has been running for over 140 years and attracts both visitors and locals. It features harness racing, ox and tractor pulls, nightly country music, woodsmen's day with ax-throwing and cross-cut saw contests and a farm museum. The fairgrounds are on Route 5. Also in Fryeburg on Route 302 is an information center operated by the Maine Publicity Bureau, open through mid-October.

One way to see the mountain colors is from a canoe seat and the Saco River near **Brownfield** offers some of the finest flatwater canoeing around. There are a number of outfitters nearby. Saco Bound is just down the road in Conway Center, New Hampshire and they offer a full range of trips, from half-day and day trips to overnight excursions with wilderness camping by the river. In Brownfield, just south of Fryeburg, River Run Canoe Rental also offers rentals, shuttles and camping.

I've canoed this stretch of the Saco and found the gentle waters perfect for a day of paddling. On one trip, I followed a stream from the river into **Pleasant Pond**, a secluded body of water with an undeveloped shoreline. Beyond the lowlands around the pond, mountains can be seen and I took picture after a picture.

A loon surfaced near the boat and I turned my camera on it, trying to capture its beauty on film. It would dive for fish and I'd try and guess where it would surface – always guessing wrong.

The loons are voracious eaters and they are capable of staying underwater for three minutes to catch minnows, though the typical dive is about 45 seconds. The bird's torpedo-like body and webbed feet propel it at great speed. Few people realize the loon is also a fast flyer, capable of traveling up to 100 miles per hour. One of the reasons you don't see loons on small bodies of water is that they need long "runs" across the surface before take-off; its ascent is quite gradual.

In Maine, the loons tend to gather at some of the larger lakes before beginning the southern migration to stay ahead of ice forming on lakes. They first travel to the coast, some even wintering off Maine, while others settle farther south along the Atlantic seaboard. The forlorn call of the loon, "the voice of the wilderness," is seldom heard from wintering birds; loon lover's like myself must wait for spring.

# Hiram

From Brownfield, one can drive south along the river following Route 5/113 to Hiram. By turning onto River Road in Hiram, you can poke along the west side of the Saco and explore more natural places. **Mount Cutler** has a trail to its summit that passes an old gold mine, a picnic area and open ledges with a view of the village below. From the railroad tracks to the summit is about three-quarters of a mile. Nearby is the Hiram Nature Study Area, which offers self-guiding trails through the woods and along the river.

# Porter

When you reach Cornish, go west on Route 25, passing through the crossroads town of Kezar Falls, and proceed on to Porter. By turning south on Route 160, you will see an old covered bridge spanning the Ossipee River. **The Parsonfield-Porter Historic Bridge**, built in 1876, is now closed to traffic, making it perfect for close inspection. When I walked through it, I ran my hand along an arch that was comprised of 21 separate curved planks bolted together. At an opening in the bridge, I looked out at the river flowing below and could see a downstream riffle. I stayed a moment, wondering if trout were holding at the edge of the fast water. Tree swallows glided just above the water's surface and the peacefulness of the place seemed to bring me back to a simpler time. I could almost hear the creak of wagon wheels echoing over the bridge's wooden planking.

An interesting day trip can be made from Fryeburg by heading north on Route 5 and going to the Bethel/Grafton Notch State Park region. The ride up Route 5 has some scenic views. Maine writer Mike Corrigan describes **Center Lovell,** which you pass through, as "a graceful line of homes" and the adjacent Slab City Road as "yet another wonderful back road." He and I both love the old farmhouses that seem to be "set in the landscape." When you reach Bethel, follow the Androscoggin River northeastward via Route 5, then make a side trip up Sunday River Road in **Newry** to see Maine's most painted and photographed covered bridge. Because of its beauty, it has been nicknamed the "Artist's Bridge," but the real name of this structure, built in 1872, is simply the **Sunday River Bridge**.

I love this spot, making a point to stop here and swim if I'm in the area in the summer. The river is beautiful, clear and cold, flowing southeast through dark hills of conifers. Certain rivers can grow on you and I'm reminded of a poignant passage written by author and poet James Dickey:

*The river and everything I remembered about it became
a possession to me, a personal, private possession,
as nothing else in my life ever had. Now it ran nowhere
but in my head, but there it ran as though immortality....
In me it still is and will be until I die, green, rocky,
deep, fast, slow and beautiful beyond reality.*

Nearby is **Grafton Notch State Park**, one of Maine's top areas for hiking. It can be reached by following Route 5 northeast from Sunday River Road a couple miles and then turning onto Route 26 north. Up the road a few miles, just north of Newry, is a series of unique geological sites, all marked by signs. Screw Auger Falls Gorge has cascading water filling shallow pools and a trail which leads down to the small meandering gorge. There is a picnic area close to the road. Mother Walker Falls Gorge, just up the road a piece, also has trails along the V-shaped gorge and features a natural stone bridge. At Moose Cave Gorge is a 200-foot-long crack in the bedrock near the 40-foot gorge. Well-maintained trails take you by large mossy boulders in shaded woods.

If it's mountain climbing you are after, **Old Speck Mountain** (also off Route 26) is the state's third highest mountain and the four-mile trail is challenging. The Eyebrow Trail is a side trail which leads to a part of the Grafton Notch wall called Eyebrow Sheer Cliff. Table Rock features a one-mile climb up **Baldpate Mountain**. At the summit is a flat ledge with rock slabs that form caves. There are excellent views of Grafton Notch, which is spectacular during peak foliage.

## For More Information
*(Area code 207 unless noted otherwise)*

| | |
|---|---|
| Bridgton Historical Society | ☎ 647-8575 |
| Fryeburg Fair | ☎ 935-3268 |
| Grafton Notch State Park (statewide) | ☎ 585-2261 |
| Jones Museum | ☎ 787-3370 |

| | |
|---|---|
| Naples Flying Service | ☎ 693-6591 |
| River Run Canoe Rental | ☎ 452-2500 |
| Saco Bound | ☎ 603-447-2177 |
| Sebago Lake State Park | ☎ 963-6321 |
| *Songo River Queen II* | ☎ 693-6861 |

# For Accommodations
### *(Area code 207 unless noted otherwise)*

**In Bridgton**

| | |
|---|---|
| Arey's Highland Lake Motel | ☎ 647-5407 |
| Blue Goose Motor Court | ☎ 647-3337 |
| Bridgton Chamber of Commerce<br>Cottage Rentals | ☎ 647-3472 |
| Bridgton Pines Cabins | ☎ 647-8227 |
| Country Crosby Motel & Cottage | ☎ 647-3426 |
| First and Last Resort | ☎ 647-2200 |
| Grady's West Shore Motel | ☎ 647-2284 |
| Merryfield Cove Cottages & Guest Rooms | ☎ 647-2847 |
| Morgansleben Lodge | ☎ 647-5066 |
| Noble House Bed and Breakfast | ☎ 647-3733 |
| Tarry-A-While Resort On Highland Lake | ☎ 647-2522 |

**In Brownfield**

| | |
|---|---|
| Alecia's Bed and Breakfast | ☎ 935-3969 |

**In Cornish**

| | |
|---|---|
| Cornish Inn | ☎ 625-8501 |
| Mid-Way Motel | ☎ 625-8835 |

**In Fryeburg**

| | |
|---|---|
| Admiral Peary House | ☎ 935-3365 |
| Jockey Cap Motel | ☎ 935-2306 |
| Oxford House Inn | ☎ 935-3442 |
| The Country Inn | ☎ 935-3334 |

**In Naples**

| | |
|---|---|
| Augusta Bove House Bed and Breakfast | ☎ 693-6365 |
| Country Sleigh | ☎ 693-6753 |
| Inn at Long Lake | ☎ 693-6226 |
| outside Maine | ☎ 800-437-0328 |
| Lambs Mill Inn | ☎ 693-6253 |
| Romah Motor Inn | ☎ 693-6690 |
| West Shore Motel | ☎ 693-9277 |

**In Sebago**
    Anderson's Motel & Cottages      ☎ 787-2477
    Goodwin's Lodge & Cottages      ☎ 787-2101
    Hostage Sports      ☎ 787-3137
**In Standish**
    Sebago Lake Resort      ☎ 787-3671

# The Kennebec River Valley

## Bingham to The Forks & Beyond

 To reach the Kennebec River Valley from I-95, take exit 36 at Waterville onto Route 201 north and proceed toward Bingham and Moscow. Peak foliage: the last few days of Sept. and the first week of Oct.

**Highlights:** *Waterfalls, rafting, canoeing, moose watching, unusual museum, hiking, colorful history and hilltops.*

In 1775, Benedict Arnold and 1,100 fellow Patriots marched up the Kennebec River Valley to storm Quebec during the American Revolutionary War. This is a story of incredible hardship and courage. Using bateaux (high-sided, double-ended boats), they struggled upriver, often carrying the heavy boats over uncharted wilderness, with starvation sapping their strength. The made it to Quebec, but their gallant assault failed. The survivors had to cross back through Maine, this time in winter's icy grip, to return home.

As I write this, we are retracing a portion of Arnold's journey and it seems almost sinful to be enjoying the area. After exploring, we have decided to focus our trip on the upper part of the Kennebec River Valley, from Bingham to The Forks, where Route 201 hugs the river and winds over hills to the Great North Woods. This ramble is in a remote region where you must have an eye for nature's beauty to fully enjoy it. If waterfalls, moose, rafting, or canoeing interest you, this is the place. The area is often overlooked by others and, even during peak foliage season, the roads are still relatively free of traffic.

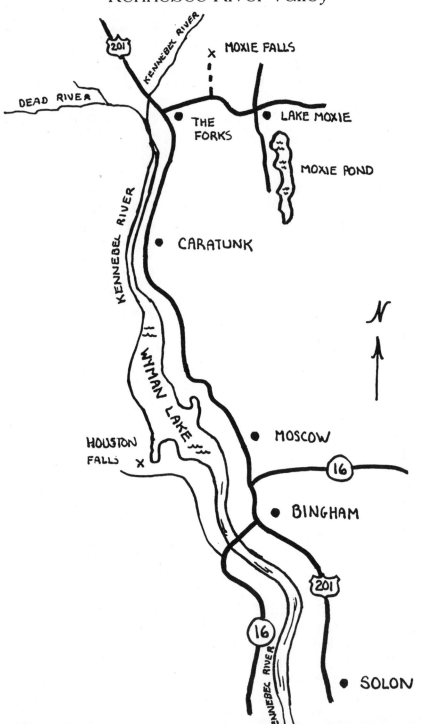

# Kennebec River Valley

# Wyman Lake
# (Moscow & Bingham)

Just north of the little neighboring villages of Moscow and Bingham is Wyman Lake, an impoundment on the Kennebec created when Central Maine Power built a huge dam in 1920. It is here that a visitor to the region gets a first sweeping view of both mountains and water. For a closer look at the lake, visit the small park at the **Wyman Lake Recreation Area** on the western shore (signs will direct you there from the center of Bingham). Along the way, you will pass a number of white birches with golden foliage standing in stark contrast to the blue waters of the bordering lake.

The recreation area is a good picnic spot, but an even better one lies just a short distance farther ahead at **Houston Brook Falls**. Look for a sign on the right side of the road, then follow the trail downward, bearing left. After only a five-minute walk you will emerge from the shade of the forest to sunlight at the base of the falls, where the photo opportunities are excellent.

If you are here in early September, it may just be warm enough to take a dip in the clear pool and let the falling water give you a first-class back massage. There are trails leading to the top of the falls as well as another that follows the brook downstream to Wyman Lake. Along the trails are hobblebush shrubs, whose foliage begins to turn color by mid-summer. You will recognize it by its large round leaves that have bright hues of yellow, orange and maroon. Hobblebush is a Viburnum; moosewood is the common name. As it implies, moose browse the hobblebush and there are plenty of moose in the region to do just that. (Locals tell me that near The Forks, north of Lake Wyman, moose are often seen on the road to Lake Moxie, which also makes a good leaf-peeping ramble.)

Moose are plentiful in this area, so drive carefully, especially at dusk and during the night, when they are most active. Other wildlife you might encounter includes white-tailed deer, partridge, fox, coyote and maybe even black bear. Bald eagles are some-times seen cruising above the Kennebec, so it's a good idea to travel with a pair of binoculars. The fishing is good and there are some nice brookies in the numerous streams that roll off the mountains to feed the Kennebec. Rainbow trout are established in the Kennebec River and one- to three-pounders have been caught.

The area, however, is best known as the **whitewater rafting center** of the northeast. The rafting began in 1976 when a fishing guide who rafted the river realized that many customers enjoyed the raft ride as much as the fishing. Today, there are several rafting outfitters that carry over 30,000 visitors each season down the river from Indian Pond, through the Kennebec Gorge to The Forks. The excursions here are for thrill-seekers with Class IV and V rapids flowing through this wild section of river. September and early October provide some the best rafting because of good water flows, uncrowded rivers and spectacular foliage. Many outfitters offer canoe and kayak instructions and river trips in a slow-paced environment. Mountain biking, nature walks and rock climbing are also available.

Some of the rafting companies offer lodging. The **Crab Apple Acres Inn** and the **Sterling Inn** are notable because they welcome non-rafters. Both are located right on Route 201. The Crab Apple Inn is a 19th-century farmhouse with guest rooms. It also serves as the headquarters for **Crab Apple Rafting**. Next to the inn is a log lodge, built in 1987, which has private guest rooms.

The Sterling Inn is more upscale than most of the other lodging facilities in the area, with a cozy feel and tastefully decorated rooms. This bed and breakfast evokes the easy pace of a Maine sporting lodge at the turn of the century and the large country porch and central gathering room are great places to relax and meet fellow guests. The inn is associated with the **New England Whitewater Center**, which offers overnight trips on the river, day hikes on the Appalachian Trail, exploration of wilderness lakes by canoe and nature walks with their resident naturalist.

Besides the inns mentioned (and the many campgrounds owned by various rafting companies), there are other bed and breakfasts as well as cabins, such as **Chadbourne's Wyman Lake Cabins**, right on the shore of Wyman Lake. Owner Sandy Chadbourne, with her three sons, has been running the business for the past 10 years and guests love the friendly atmosphere. Mark and I stayed in a cabin just 20 feet from the water's edge and spent considerable time on the front porch, reading, writing and just plain soaking up the peace of the lake. We also took a long paddle in one of Sandy's canoes, heading south to a small wooded island where we beached the canoe and braved the chilly waters for a invigorating dip.

**Canoeing** on Wyman Lake is as tranquil as can be, largely because there is so little development along the shoreline. Hills frame the lake and yellow, orange and red foliage reflect on the water. One section of the western shoreline was especially colorful with poplar, birch, oak and maple branching out over the light gray and brown stones that dot the shore. Dark green hemlocks are intermixed with the hardwoods; twisted driftwood, bleached white, adds further contrast.

Besides paddling Wyman Lake or riding the river to soak up fall's colors, try a hike up **Pleasant Pond Mountain**, where the Appalachian Trail crosses its summit. Sweeping views offer a panorama of rust-colored hills dotted with shining blue ponds. Moosehead Lake, Mount Kineo and Sugarloaf are just some of the landmarks seen from the top. The hike to the top is a strenuous 1.4-mile climb up steep terrain. It takes about an hour, so be sure to leave early and carry water. To reach the trail, turn off Route 201 at Caratunk and follow the road to Pleasant Pond. When you reach a fork in the road by the pond and the Dew Drop Inn, bear left and follow it past Fire Road #10 to a parking area straight ahead. At the summit, there is a ledge with a 360°

view. Wild blueberry bushes will dazzle you with their scarlet leaves.

One of Maine's most spectacular sights, especially in autumn, is **Moxie Falls**, off the road to Lake Moxie out of The Forks. The hike into the falls is on a well-marked trail and takes about 15 minutes. The woodland scents of ferns and moss rise up to greet you on this shaded walk and the hemlocks are offset by the color of white birch, silver birch and maples. When you first get a glimpse of a small falls and the rushing stream, you might think you see Moxie Falls, but push on a few more feet. Soon you will hear the unmistakable roar of giant Moxie Falls, the highest in New England. Stairways and observation platforms have been installed for safety and to control erosion. The viewing platform at the main falls is perfect for photographs and there is a very steep fisherman's trail that leads to the base of the falls.

Mark and I were content to stay at the observation platform, snapping photos of the falls and surrounding color. But somehow, pictures never fully capture the vividness of color or the full drama of the falls, so we ended up just watching and listening. Hiking out from the falls is mostly uphill and had me a little winded, reminding me of the Robert Frost poem *A Leaf-Treader*, "I have been treading on leaves all day until I am autumn tired."

# Jackman

Mark and I ended our trip at Moxie Falls, but you might want to follow Route 201 to Jackman. Years ago, I traveled through Jackman and spent a few days on majestic **Moosehead Lake** and I've wanted to come back ever since and take an autumn boat ride on its waters. If you leave The Forks and travel northwest on Route 201, you will have the pleasure of seeing the **Attean Overlook**, five miles south of Jackman. The spectacular view is of the island-dotted Attean Pond and the westward hills that stretch toward the Canadian border – an especially breathtaking vista at sunset. From Jackman, the intrepid traveler could take

Route 15 eastward to Moosehead Lake at the town of Rockwood and then head south to Greenville.

# Hinckley

If you are heading back to Interstate 95 after your ramble, consider stopping at the **L.C. Bates Museum** on Route 201 in Hinckley. The museum is filled with a strange hodgepodge of exhibits: an alligator skull, fossils, sculptures, hundreds of stuffed birds, Indian artifacts and even a Gila monster. There are antique cabinets of glass and golden oak housing objects from around the world and there are theme rooms, such as the one that features a collection of marine life with fish, shells and corals. Of special interest to children, the natural-history exhibits feature bobcat, bear and fox displayed in their natural habitats, with painted backgrounds by Mr. Charles Hubbard, a well-known American impressionist.

# Norridgewock

Tree enthusiasts may want to detour off Route 201 into Norridgewock and take Route 8 south for half a mile to Martin Stream Road. By following this country lane 1.8 miles, you will see the **Ashley Wing Memorial Park** on the left. By taking the trail to the left as you face the woods, it's only a two-minute walk to one of the Pine Tree State's largest white pines.

## For More Information
*(Area code 207 unless noted otherwise)*

| | |
|---|---|
| Crab Apple Whitewater Rafting | ☎ 800-553-7238 |
| Kennebec Valley Tourism Council | ☎ 800-778-9898 |

L.C. Bates Museum     ☎ 397-2004
Moosehead Lake Region Chamber     ☎ 695-2702
  of Commerce
North Country Rivers     ☎ 800-348-8871
Raft Maine     ☎ 800-359-2106 or 824-3694
Upper Kennebec Valley Chamber     ☎ 672-4100
  of Commerce

# For Accommodations
*(Area code 207 unless noted otherwise)*

**In Moscow**
Chadbourne's Wyman Lake Cabins     ☎ 672-3771
**In Bingham**
Bingham Motor Inn     ☎ 800-439-4135 or 672-4135
Mrs. G's B & B     ☎ 672-4034
Pine Grove Lodge Bed and Breakfast     ☎ 672-4011
**In Caratunk**
The Sterling Inn     ☎ 672-5506
**In The Forks**
Crab Apple Acres Inn     ☎ 800-553-7238

# Coastal Maine, Penobscot Peninsula

 Take I-95 to Bangor exit 45 onto I-395. Cross the Penobscot River and get onto State Route 15 heading south along the river toward Bucksport. This trip explores the towns, villages and scenic roads of the Penobscot Peninsula down to Stonington on Deer Isle. Peak foliage expected: September 25-October 11th.

> **Highlights:** *Scenic coastal roads, coves and harbors, the historic towns of Blue Hill, Castine and the old fishing village of Stonington.*

Fall may come in many varied forms and its colors may be found in more than just trees. For a change from the majestic mountains of Vermont and New Hampshire, treat yourself to a exploratory journey along the Maine coast. Here, among the rocky bays, scenic peninsulas, gentle hills, fields and woodlands the colors are rich and deep, subtle and vibrant. Here, autumn can be found among the orange and ochre grasses, the crimson blueberry fields, the deep ultramarine sky reflected in ponds, bays and harbors. There is even color in the many rocks and boulders found in every cove. And if it's trees you can't live without, there are plenty of those here too. In fact, more than half of your drives between towns will be through dense wooded areas, which, if you come at the right time, can explode with color. The variety of trees here may surprise you as well as you pass birch, oak, maple, larch, poplar, evergreens and even elms. Don't worry about being closed in by trees all the time, there are plenty of views too, which look across the waters and fields as far as the eye can see.

# Coastal Maine

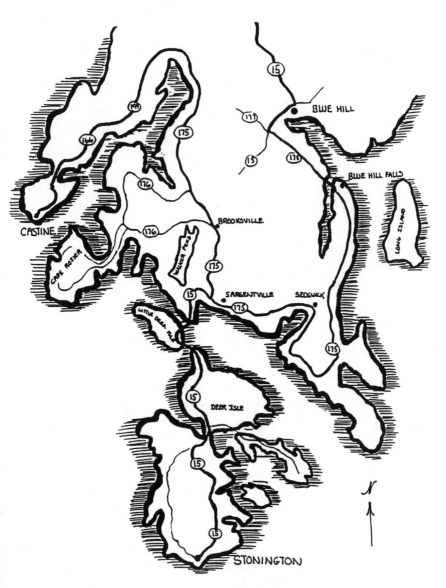

For me, exploring the coast of Maine for the first time was exhilarating. I had traveled, camped, hiked and canoed in some of the interior regions in the past, but the coast is an entirely different 'picture.' A trip to the Maine coast should not be missed; there are hundreds of places you could go and not be disappointed. Many tourists make it up to the Bar Harbor area, which is just south of here. Easy access to the adjacent Acadia National Park is one of the big draws – and for good reason. You may want to go there as well, but you will probably encounter more travelers. If you enjoy solitude, head north of Bar Harbor and beyond. The Penobscot area offers a good balance between the two. The roads are not jammed and there are plenty of quiet places to take an isolated walk along the shore. Yet there is also a good range of accommodations, restaurants, shops and attractions.

A good map of the area will be of tremendous help, especially if you want to explore some the side roads. When Mike and I took this trip we traveled the coastal roads, such as State Route 175 from Blue Hill to Sargentville and State Route 176 around the Brooksville area. We traversed many of the interior roads and also drove out to some of the smaller peninsulas (the Sunshine Road on Stinson Neck near Deer Isle village was a good one). To give you an idea of size, it takes about an hour and 30 minutes to drive – without stopping – from the town of Orland in the north to Stonington on the outermost tip of Deer Isle. If you stay in the area for a couple of nights you should have enough time to explore without feeling hurried.

# Blue Hill

The town of Blue Hill may be your first stop on the peninsula, and it's a good one. Going back as a village to at least 1762, Blue Hill depended on ship building and the sea trade for its livelihood. Between 1792 and 1882 over 133 vessels were built here, most of which were schooners. As the ship-building industry declined, mining began to take over the town around 1879, followed by the granite industry. By 1907 there were six quarries in town. It was also around this time that city people began arriving for the summer, many of whom loved it enough to stay on year-round.

The town center is ripe for walking and enjoying the shops and scenery. You can't miss the beautiful old town hall in the center, set upon a small hill surrounded by elms and maples. Diagonally across the street is the **Holt House**, built in 1815 and now home to the Blue Hill Historical Society. Make sure you walk down the adjacent Water Street to take in the view of this very picturesque harbor. The town is also known for its concentration of artists, musicians and writers and you are sure to come across several galleries as you explore the main roads in town. I particularly enjoyed the **Lirds Gallery**, on Main Street, and **Belchers Antiques and Gifts**, on Water Street.

Just outside of town on State Route 175 going south, take a look at the **Blue Hills Falls**. Niagara it is not, but its back tidal current allows kayakers to remain stationary as they play the water facing upstream. You may be able to watch a few of them practice their skills.

State Route 175 will appear surprisingly undeveloped. Most of the homes are on the water's edge and many are hidden from view down long driveways. You can get a nice view of Herrick Bay from the road near Brooklin; farther on at Sedgwick the road follows the Benjamin River, offering more water views. Old white homes and colorful maples reflect upon the water's surface as State Route 175 takes you along both sides of the mouth of this river which connects to the elongated Salt Pond just south of Blue Hill.

Several miles on, the **Caterpillar Hill** area between Sargentville and Brooksville offers some of the best views around. You will be able to see across and down to Walker Pond and the Eggemoggin Reach beyond. Much of the hillside here is covered by blueberry bushes which in autumn turn from green to a brilliant crimson. The far-reaching panoramic view is fabulous and, fortunately, there is a rest stop so you can pull the car over and enjoy it.

From Brooksville, I recommend you take State Route 176 past South Brooksville – where there are some good harbor views – and go out to **Cape Rosier**. Look for the left-hand turn onto

Cape Rosier Road. The **Holbrook Sanctuary** offers hiking and Goose Falls. This is a dirt road that eventually becomes paved. Just follow the coast, bearing right, and you will eventually pass the large Bayside Lodge. This is a wonderful stretch of road, with the ocean to one side and hills and fields on the other. It seemed like a great area to be traveling on a bike, so keep it in mind when you pack your car. If you stay on the outer road you will arrive at the small **Bakeman Beach**, a nice spot for a picnic and a good place to stretch the old legs.

# Castine

At some point in your explorations you should head for Castine. It's a pleasant enough drive from Cape Rosier and you will enjoy some of the old farms and buildings, such as the West Brooksville Congregational Church built in 1855. Head down toward Castine via State Route 166, which will take you right into the center of town.

Named after a French soldier, Castine's known history goes back as far as 1604 when Samuel de Champlain came ashore here. Starting off as a trading post, Castine's history becomes complex as the town changed hands many times, complete with invasions and small battles. It was owned at one time by French, Dutch and English. You can even explore the remains of Fort George, which was built by the British in 1779 on the peninsula's highest point. The rest of Castine's history is similar to that of Blue Hill. That is, after 1800 the town expanded rapidly as ship building prospered and the harbor began to grow in importance. The town became one of the wealthiest per capita and continued to prosper until the Civil War as ship building was replaced by the railroad boom. But by the turn of the century, wealthy summer visitors began to come, many of whom eventually helped to restore the multitude of old homes as well as build their own.

Drive down to the town dock and leave your car in the large parking lot. You can't miss the enormous training ship anchored here, which is used by the Maine Maritime Academy. The Academy makes its home here in Castine and it's most likely you will pass it as you enter the town. Take the time to walk some of Castine's beautiful streets. With its countless historic homes, many of them formerly belonging to sea captains, it is a walk you won't forget.

The **John Perkins House** on Perkins Street was built in 1665 and is the oldest one in town. (It has actually been moved from its original location on Court Street.) The **Wilson Museum** is also on Perkins Street and is open through September. It houses artifacts, old farming equipment and an 1805 kitchen. The hearse house and blacksmith shop are also on the grounds. There are far too many historic homes to mention here, but a list of them is provided on the excellent town map available at the information booth near the training ship.

Above all, I think it is the elm trees that really make Castine so beautiful and unique. These large and graceful trees line the main streets of town. Their slender and tapering limbs hang down, perfectly framing the old white homes. This is indeed a rare sight, for most of the elms in New England succumbed to Dutch elm disease years ago. These elms were saved, however, due to the deliberate and careful efforts of those who believed they were worth saving and had the know-how and means to do so. Walking down the shaded streets of Castine, one gets an idea of what many towns might have looked liked before the disease took hold.

There are two "isles" just south of the peninsula, both of them connected by State Route 15. As you leave Sargentville you will cross over the first bridge to Little Deer Isle; "little" is the key word here. There's not a whole lot to explore here as most of the views are on private property. Better to keep on going over the next causeway onto **Deer Isle**. Once here you can explore (again, you'll want a good map) some of the side roads, such as Reach Road, which will lead you to a few coves. The first town you'll come to is Deer Isle – worth peeking at – but it's **Ston-ington** that attracts the most attention.

# Stonington

State Route 15 will bring you directly into the downtown area and you'll probably want to park the car as soon as possible and get out and walk, which is exactly what we did. Few can deny that the physical layout of this old fishing town is extraordinary in its beauty and classic in its design. Unlike the more pristine Castine, Stonington, being a working fishing village, has a few rough edges, but herein lies its appeal. It has retained its original flavor, from the rising and falling streets down to the aging piers and docks within the cove. If you have an artist's or photographer's eye, you should be more than satisfied as the town offers one superb composition after the next. You can spend a good afternoon exploring the harbor area as well as the streets that make their way uphill. Looking down over the rooftops and out across the bay is one of the most memorable views at any time of year. On a clear autumn day, however, the light and colors are dazzling to the eye.

You will probably want to spend at least one night here, and there are several bed and breakfasts near the center of town. Mike and I were fortunate enough to get a room at the **Burnt Cove Bed and Breakfast**, which overlooks Burnt Cove just outside of town. This is the home of Diane Berlew and Bob Williams, who built the house on land once owned by Bob's father. It's a quiet spot with a great view and the architecture is open and spacious. Bob (who is a lifelong resident and fisherman) and Diane know the area and history well and could certainly give you some tips on visiting the area.

Remember, peak foliage time is fairly difficult to pin down along the coast here and it can be spotty. However, any time during September or October would be highly recommended.

# For More Information
*(Area code 207)*

| | |
|---|---|
| Belcher's Antiques and Gifts, Blue Hill | ☎ 374-5769 |
| Blue Heron Gallery, Deer Isle Village | ☎ 348-6051 |
| Castine Historical Society, Castine | ☎ 326-8786 |
| Crockett Cove Woods Trails, Deer Isle | ☎ 729-5181 |
| Eaton's Pier Restaurant, Deer Isle | ☎ 348-2489 |
| Fisherman's Friend Restaurant, Stonington | ☎ 367-2442 |
| Haystack Mtn School of Crafts, Deer Isle | ☎ 348-2306 |
| Holt House Historical Society, Blue Hill | ☎ 374-5485 |
| Jonathan Fisher Mem. Museum | ☎ 374-2161 |
| Island Historical Society, Deer Isle | ☎ 348-2886 |
| Liros Gallery Inc., Blue Hill | ☎ 374-5370 |
| Penobscot Marine Museum, Searsport | ☎ 548-2529 |
| Salome Sellers House, Deer Isle | ☎ 367-5012 |
| Wilson Museum | *no listing* |

# For Accommodations
*(Area code 207)*

**In Castine**

| | |
|---|---|
| Castine Inn | ☎ 326-4365 |
| Pentagoet Inn | ☎ 326-8616 |

**In Blue Hill**

| | |
|---|---|
| Blue Hill Farm Country Inn | ☎ 374-5126 |
| Blue Hill Inn | ☎ 374-2844 |

**In Deer Isle**

| | |
|---|---|
| Deer Isle Village Inn | ☎ 348-2564 |
| The Bridge Inn Restaurant & Motel, Little Deer Isle | ☎ 348-6115 |

**In Stonington**

| | |
|---|---|
| Burnt Cove Bed & Breakfast | ☎ 367-2392 |

# Index

CONNECTICUT, 1-36

Accommodations, *22,35*
Appalachian Trail, *32*

Bald Peak, *33*
Bantam Village, *26*
Bear Mountain, *33*
Blake, Noah, *29*
Boulder Inn, *27*
Bowen, Henry Chandler, *21*
Brayton Gristmill, *20*
Brooklyn, *16-18*
Bulls Covered Bridge, *29*
Bunnell Farm, *25*

Canaan, *33-34*
Canterbury, *15-16*
Cathedral Pines, *30*
Chaiwalla Tea Room, *32*
Chase, Edith Morton, *23*
Christmas Barn, *21*
Churches, *15, 17, 20, 25, 27*
Collin's Diner, *33*
Cornwall Bridge Pottery, *31*
Cornwall covered bridge, *31*
Covered bridges, *29, 31*
Crandall, Prudence, House
  Museum, *15, 16*

Dennis Hill State Park, *34*
Depot Pub and Grub, *33*

East Canaan, *33-34*
1890 Colonial B&B, *31*
Ellsworth Hill Farm, *31*

Fishing, *31*
Fox Hunt Farms Gourmet, *20*

Golden Lamb at Hillandale
  Farm, *17*

Haight Vineyard, *25*
Harney & Sons Ltd., *32*

Haystack Mountain, *34*
Hopkins Inn, *27*
Hopkins Winery, *27*
Housatonic River, *28*

Indian Chair, I20
Ingersoll, Jan, Shaker Furniture
  Shop, *30*
Inn at Lake Waramaug, *27*

Kent, *29-30*
Kent Falls, *30*
Kent Iron Furnace, *30*

Lake Waramaug, *27*
Lake Waramaug State Park, *27*
Lapsley Orchards, *18*
Litchfield, *23-26*
Litchfield Food Company, *25*
Litchfield Hills, *23-36*
Lodging, *22, 35*

Mashamoquat Brook State Park,
  *18-20*
Mount Riga, *32-33*
Mount Tom Tower and Pond, *26*

New England Center for
  Contemporary Art, *18*
New Preston, *27-28*
New Milford, *28*
Norfolk, *28*
North Canaan, *33*
Northeast Audubon Center, *31*

Park Lane Cider, *28*
Pomfret, *18-20*
Putnam Elms, *17*
Putnam, General Israel, *16*
Putnam Wolf Den, *19*

Reid & Wright Antiquarian Book
  Center, *28*
Riverrunning Expeditions, *32*
Roseland Cottage, *21*

Salisbury, *32-33*
Sharon, *31*
Silo Gallery, *28*
Smith, Chard Powers, *28*
Sloane Stanley Museum, *19*
Sloane, Eric, *29, 30*

Topsmead State Forest, *23*
Tourist information, *6, 22*
Trail of the Senses, *26*

Vanilla Bean Café, *20*

Walking Weekend, *16*
West Cornwall, *31*
Whistle Stop Ice Cream
  Shop, *33*
White Flower Farm, *25*
White Memorial Conservation
  Center, *26*
Woodstock, *20-21*
Woodstock Fairgrounds, *20*
Wright's Mill Tree Farm, *16*

MAINE, 153-180

Accommodations, *163-4, 172,
  180*
Androscoggin River, *161*
Arnold, Benedict, *165*
Artist's Bridge, *see* Sunday
  River Bridge
Ashley Wing Mem. Park, *171*
Attean Overlook, *170*

Bait and Bucket, *158*
Bakeman Beach, *177*
Bates, L.C., Museum, *171*
Belchers Antiques and Gifts,
  *176*
Benjamin River, *176*
Bethel, *161*
Bingham, *167*
Blue Hill, *175-177*
Bridgton, *158-9*
Burnt Cove B&B, *179*

Canoeing, *159, 166, 168-9*
Cape Rosier, *176*
Castine, *177-8*
Caterpillar Hill, *176*

Center Lovell, *161*
Chadbourne's Wyman Lake
  Cabins, *169*
Churches, *177*
Covered bridges, *161*
Crab Apple Acres Inn and
  Rafting, *168*
Crockett Cove Woods nature
  trails, *180*

Deer Isle, *178*
Deer Isle Village, *178*
Douglas Mountain, *156*

Fishing, *158, 168*
Fryeburg, *159-160*
Fryeburg Fair, *159*

Grafton Notch State Park, *162*
Great North Woods, *165*

Hinckley, *171*
Hiram, *160*
Hiram Nature Study Area, *160*
Holbrook Sanctuary, *177*
Holt House, *176*
Houston Brook Falls, *167*

Jackman, *170-171*
Jones Museum, *157*

Kennebec River Valley, *165-172*

Little Deer Isle, *178*
Lodging, *163-4, 172, 180*
Loons, *160*

Maine Maritime Academy, *178*
Maine Publicity Bureau, *159*
Moose, *167*
Moose Cave Gorge, *162*
Moosehead Lake, *170*
Moscow, *167*
Mother Walker Falls Gorge, *162*
Mount Cutler, *160*
Moxie Falls, *170*

Naples, *158*
Naples Flying Service, *158*
Narramissic, *see* Peabody-Fitch
  Farm

# Index

New England Whitwater
Center, *168*
Newry, *161*
Norridgewock, *171*

Old Speck Mountain, *162*

Parsonfield-Porter Historic
Bridge, *161*
Peabody-Fitch Farm, *159*
Perkins, John, House, *178*
Pleasant Pond Mountain, *169*
Porter, *161-2*

Saco River, *155-6, 159*
Screw Auger Falls Gorge, *162*
Sebago Lake, *157*
Sebago Lake State Park, *158*
Songo River, *158*
*Songo River Queen II*, *158*
South Bridgton, *159*
Standish, *156*
Steep Falls, *156*
Sterling Inn, *168*
Stonington, *179*
Sunday River Bridge, *161*

Tourist information, *6, 171-2*

Whitewater rafting, *168*
Wilson Museum, *178*
Wyman Lake, *167, 169*

MASSACHUSETTS, 51-71

Accommodations, 62, 70
Ashley, Colonel, House, *67*
Ashley Falls, *67*

Bartholomew's Cobble, *67*
Barre, *60*
Bash Bish Falls, *68*
Bears Den, *57*
Beartown State Forest, *66*
Belchertown, *54*
Belchertown Annual Fair, *54*
Berkshire Botanical Garden, *69*
Bidwell House, *66*
Brooks Woodland Preserve, *59*
Buffam Falls Cons. Area, *55*
Bullard Farm, *57*

Chesterwood, *69*
Churches, *54, 59, 64*
Common Reader, *56*
Conners Pond, 60
Country Store (Petersham), *58*

Deerfield, *57*

Egremont Inn, *67*
Enfield Lookout, *54*

Fishing, *58*
French, Daniel Chester, *69*

Gaslight Store, *67*
Giant Pumpkin Contest, *59*
Gingerbread House, *see*
Tyringham Art Galleries
Goodnow Dike, *54*
Great Barrington, *66-67*

Hamilton Orchards, *55-56*
Hartman's Herb Farm, *60*
Housatonic River, *67*

Joyous Spring Pottery, *66*

Keystone Bridge, *58*
King Phillip's War, *57*

Lodging, *62, 70*

Monterey, *63-66*
Monument Mountain, *68*
Mount Washington, *68*

New Salem, *55-58*
Nipmuck Indians, *57*
North Common Meadow, *58-59*
North New Salem, *57*

Pelham, *54-55*
Petersham Center, *58*
Phillipston, *59-60*

Quabbin Reservoir, *53*
Quabbin Summit Tower, *54*

Red Lion Inn, *69*
Rock House Reservation, *61*
Rockingstone Park, *60*

# Index

Rockwell, Norman, Museum, *69*

Salem Cross Inn, *61*
Sandisfield State Forest, *66*
Serenity Hill, *56*
Shays, Daniel, *55*
South Egremont, *67-67*
Stockbridge, *69*
Stone House Museum, *54*
Sunset Farms, *64*
Swift River, *57, 58, 59*
Swift River Reservation, *59-60*

Tourist information, *6, 61, 70*
Tyringham, *63-65*
Tyringham Art Galleries, *63*
Tyringham Cobble, *64-65*

Ware, *54*
Weathervane Inn, *68*
Winsor Dam, *54*

Yankee Strudel Bakery, *57*

NEW HAMPSHIRE, 123-152

Accommodations, *133, 148, 152*
Aching Acres Farm, *126*
Appalachian Trail, *132*
Audubon Society Hawk Watch, *145*

Ball, Benjamin, *141*
Bellows Falls, *128*
Bird watching, *see* Audubon Society Hawk Watch
Blow Me Down Hill, *131*
Boggy Meadow Farm, *127-8*

Champney Falls, *152*
Charlestown, *129-130*
Charlestown Fort, *see* Fort at No. 4
Churches, *139, 140, 145*
Clay Library, *139*
Connecticut River, *125-133*
Connecticut River Bridge, *128*
Cornish, *130-132*
Cornish Colony, *130*

Cornish-Windsor covered bridge, *130*
Covered bridges, *130*
Cutler Memorial Building, *139*

Dartmouth Bookstore, *132*
Dartmouth College, *132*
Dartmouth Outing Club, *132*
Drewsville, *127-8*
Dublin, *145*

Fall foliage ride, *see* Green Mountain Railroad
Farwell School, *129*
Flint, Thomas, *127*
Fort at No. 4, *129*
Freeman, Dorcas, *140-1*
Frost Free Library, *137*

Golden Past Antiques, *126-7*
Greeley Pond Scenic Area, *151*
Green Mountain Railroad, *128*

Hancock, *140-142*
Hancock Inn, *141*
Hanover, *132*
Hanover Trails Association, *132*
Harris Center for Conservation Education, *142*
Harrisville, *146*
Homestead Bookshop, *137*
Honey Lane Farm, *145*

Jaffrey, *137-8*
Jigger Johnson Campground, *151*

Kancamagus, Chief, *149*
Kancamagus Highway, *149-152*
Keene, *137*
Kilburn, John, *128*

Lincoln, *151-2*
Lincoln Woods Trail Center, *151*
Lodging, *133, 148, 152*
Loon Mounatin Recreation Area, *150*
Loon Mountain Ski Resort, *150*
Lower Falls Recreation Center, *152*
MacDowell Colony, *142*
Marlborough, *137*

# Index

Melville Academy Building, *139*
Mill Pond, *127*
Miller State Park, *144*
Monadnock Books and
   Antiques, *145*
Mt. Kancamagus, *149*
Mt. Monadnock, *135, 138*
Mt. Monadnock State Park, *138*

Nelson, *147*
New England Marionette
   Opera, *143*
North Charlestown, *129*
Norway Hill Orchard, *142*
Norway Pond Beach, *140*
Nubanusit Brook, *146*

Otter Rocks Rest Area, *151*

Pack Monadnock Mtn., *144*
Parchment & Plate Books, *143*
Pelletier, Peter, Fine Art, *143*
Perry, Lilla Cabot, *142*
Petroglyphs, Indian, *128*
Peterborough, *142-5*
Pine Ridge Cemetery, *140*
Plainfield, *131*
Plainfield Wildflower Sanctuary,
   *131-2*
Porter, Rufus, *141*

River Valley Fine Arts, *127*
Rocky Gorge Scenic Area, *151*

Sabbaday Falls, *151*
Saint-Gaudens, Augustus, *130*
Saint-Gaudens National
   Historic Site, *130*
Seccombe Nature Park, *143*
Sharon Arts Center, *144*
Sheiling Forest, *143*
Stonewall Farm, *137*
Sugar Hill Overlook, *149-150*
Swift River, *149, 150*

Thoreau, Henry David, *138*
Toadstool Bookshop, *143*
Tourist information, *6, 147,*
   *152*

Upland Farm, *144*

Walpole, *126-7*
Westmoreland Depot, *126*
White Mountains, *149*
Wilder, Thornton, *142*

Yankee Books and Magazine, *145*

RHODE ISLAND, 37-50

Accommodations, *50*
Arcadia State Park, *42*

Bell School House, *45*

Carolina, *45*
Casey, Silas, Farm, *47*
Churches, *41, 43, 48*

Ell Pond, *41*
Exeter, *42-43*

Fishing, *48*
Four Point Canoe Outfitters, *45*

Great Swamp, *46*

Hack & Livery General Store, *45*
Hope Valley, *44-45*

John and Cindy's Harvest Acre
   Farm, *45*

Kenyon, *45*
Kenyon's Gristmill, *45*
King Phillip's War, *46-47*
Kingston, *44-45*

Lodging, *50*
Long & Ell Ponds Natural Area, *43*

Meadowbrook Herb Garden, *45*

Narragansett Bay, *47*
Narragansett Indians, *46-47, 49*
North Kingston, *47-48*

Oak Embers Campground, *42*
Old Narragansett Church, *48*
Our Kids Apple Farm, *42*

Rattlesnake Ledge, *40*

Richmond, *45-47*
Rockville, *43-44*
Rockville Upper Mill (Stone
  Mill), *43*

Shannock, *45*
Smith's Castle, *49*
Stepping Stone Falls, *43*
Stepping Stone Ranch, *42*
Stuart, Gilbert, *48*
Stuart, Gilbert, House and Mill,
  *48*

Tourist information, *6, 49*

Uspuepaug, *45*

West Greenwich, *40-42*
West Greenwich Church, *41*
West's Bakery, *44*
Wickaboxet State Forest, *40*
Wickford, *48-49*
Williams, Roger, *49*
Wyoming, *45*

VERMONT, 71-122

Accommodations, *86, 96-97,
  111, 121-2*
Albany, *117*
Allen, Ira, *118*
Apple Barn, *82*
Apple Days Festival, *74*
Apple & Harvest Festival, *82*
Applebrook Farms, *107*
Arlington, *81*

Barr Hill Nature Preserve, *115*
Barre, *95*
Bartleby's Book and Music
  Store, *83*
Barton, *120*
Bear Pond Books, *101*
Ben & Jerry's Ice Cream Fac-
  tory, *101*
Bennington, *82-83*
Bennington Monument, *82*
Bennington Museum, *82*
Berardinelli's General Store,
  *107*
Bethel, *90*

Bike Vermont, *90*
Billings Farm and Museum, *92*
Black Mountain Antique Center,
  *174*
Bondville, *78-79*
Boswell Botany Trail, *80*
Brattleboro, *74-75*
Brattleboro Museum and Art
  Center, *74*
Bread and Puppet Theater, *121*
Brewster River Gristmill, *102*
Brick Tavern Bed & Breakfast, *76*
Bridgewater, *91*
Brookfield, *89-90*
Brookfield Floating Bridge, *89*
Brownington Center, *119*
Browns River, *108*
Bryan, Mary, Memorial Art
  Gallery, *103*
Buttermilk Falls, *92*

Cambridge, *110*
Cambridge General Store, *110*
Canoeing, *83, 117*
Caspian Lake, *115*
Chelsea, *95*
Churches, *83, 103, 117*
Clarke Galleries, *101*
Cold Hollow Cider Mill, *101*
Coolidge, Calvin, *91*
Coolidge Birthplace and
  Homestead, *91*
Covered bridges, *74, 76, 77, 81,
  87, 90, 94, 95, 103, 104, 110*
Conaway, Jay, Art Center, *80*
Craftsbury, *116*
Craftsbury Center, *117*
Craftsbury Common, *117*
Crystal Lake State Park, *120*

Dana House Museum, *92*
Deerfield River, *83*
Dog River, *87, 89*
Dorset, *80-81*

East Craftsbury, *116-7*
Emerald Lake State Park, *80*
Equinox Hotel, *79*
Equinox Mountain Inn, *81*
Equinox Village Shops, *81*
Essex, *108*

# Index

Fairfield, *105-6*
Fairfield Center School, *105*
Fairfield Hill, *105*
Fall Foliage train ride, *110*
Falls General Store, *87*
Farmers' Market, *74*
Fishing, *78, 83, 108, 109*

Gallery North Star, *76*
Gifford Woods State Park, *90*
Giorgetti Covered Bridge, *90*
Glover, *121*
Grafton, *76-77*
Grafton Village Cheese
  Company, *76*
Green Mountain Flagship
  Company, Ltd., *83*
Green Trails Inn, *89*
Greensboro, *115*

Hard'ack Recreational Area,
  *106*
Hardwick, *115-6*
Harriman Reservoir, *83*
Helen Day Art Center, *101*
Hildene, *79*
Hogback Mountain Lookout, *84*
Howe Bridge, *94*
Hope Cemetery, *95*

Inn at Buck Hollow Farm, *107*
Inn on the Common, *117*
Irasburg, *117-120*
Irasburg Affair, *119*

Jamaica, *77-78*
Jamaica State Park, *78*
Jana's Cupboard, *103*
Jeffersonville, *102-3*
Jeff's Maine Seafood, *106*
Jericho, *108*

Killington Ski Area, *90-91*
Kill Kare State Park, *106*

Lake Champlain, *105*
Lake Willoughby, *119*
Lamoille Valley Railroad, *110*
Le Cheval d'Ors, *103*
Lincoln, Robert Todd, *79*
Locust Brook, *91*

Lodging, *86, 96-97, 111, 121-2*
Ludlow, *91*

Manchester, *79-80*
Matteson, Peter, Tavern, *82*
Mettawee River, *80*
Mill covered bridge, *94*
Montpelier, *87*
Moore Free Library (Newfane), *75*
Morrisville, *110*
Mount Equinox, *81*
Mount Mansfield, *102*
Mount Pisgah, *120*

Nepco Picnic Area, *84*
Newfane, *75*
Northeast Kingdom, *113-122*
Northfield Falls, *87-89*
Northshire Bookstore, *79*

October Country Inn, *92*
Old Red Mill, *108*
Old Red Mill Inn, *84*
Old Stone House Museum, 119

Pette Memorial Library, *83*
Pico Ski Area, *90-91*
Pittsfield, *90*
Pleasant Valley, *109*
Plymouth Cheese Factory, *91*
Plymouth Notch Historic District,
  *91*
Plymouth Union, *91*

Quilts by Elaine, *103*

Rathdowney Herbs, *90*
Robinson, Theodore, *117*
Rock of Ages Quarry, *95*
Rockwell, Norman, *81*
Rockwell, Norman, Museum, *81*
Royalton Raid, *93*

St. Albans, *106-7*
St. Albans Bay, *106*
St. Albans Historical Museum, *106*
Scott covered brudge, *77*
Shaftsbury, *82*
Shaftsbury State Park, *82*
Shire Inn, *95*
Silver Wing Art Gallery, *103*

# Index

Skyline Drive, *81*
Skyline Restaurant, *84*
Smuggler's Notch, *102*
Smuggler's Notch Inn, *103*
South Royalton, *93-94*
South Royalton House, *94*
South Vermont Art Center, *79*
Stowe, *99-102*
Stowe Foliage Craft Fair, *101*
Stowe Recreation Path, *101*
Stratton Mountain, *78*
Stratton Mountain Arts Festival, *78*
Stratton Mountain Resort, *78*

Tourist information, *6, 85-86, 96, 110-1, 121*
Townshend, *76-77*
Townshend Common, *76*
Townshend Dam, *76*
Tunbridge, *94-95*
Tunbridge World's Fair, *94*

Underhill, *109*

Underhill Annual Harvest Market, *109*
Underhill State Park, *109*

Vermont Raptor Center, *93*
Vermont Maple Outfit, *110*
Village Restaurant, *115*

Waterville, *104-5*
West Dummerston, *74*
West River, *74, 77, 78*
Westford, *107-8*
White River, *90, 93*
White River National Fish Hatchery, *90*
Wilder House, *91*
Wilder Barn, *91*
Willoughby State Forest, *120*
Wilmington, *83-84*
Windham Brewery, *74*
Windham Foundation, *76*
Windridge Bakery, *103*
Woodford State Park, *82*
Woodstock, *92-93*